Discursions on Travel, Art and Life

MARIA CRISTINA, QUEEN OF NAPLES, AT CASERTA

(From the painting by Carlo dè Falco)

DISCURSIONS

ON
TRAVEL, ART AND LIFE

BY

OSBERT SITWELL

GREENWOOD PRESS, PUBLISHERS
WESTPORT, CONNECTICUT

Originally published in 1925
by Grant Richards, Ltd., London

First Greenwood Reprinting 1970

Library of Congress Catalogue Card Number 70-109844

SBN 8371-4336-5

Printed in the United States of America

Preface

IT is with yet more than his usual diffidence that the author begs to present these "Discursions" to the public. But since volumes of travel are his favourite books, and travelling, rather than golf or hunting, his chosen form of exercise and sport, he will be perfectly satisfied if they communicate some of the pleasure himself has experienced to the gentle reader. Nor, in his opinion, is it enough to describe the things seen; for one of the chief virtues of travel is that it enables the mind to voyage more easily, even, than the body, to move backward and forward through time as well as in space. At one moment the traveller is able to measure the dome of St Peter's in Rome by that of St Paul's in London, at another to contemplate the march of the Roman Legions and compare it with that of the passing Fascisti. He can flit from Italy to Spain, from architecture to music. For travel is like a drug that permeates the mind with an indefinite but unusual tinge, stimulating and releasing, imparting a greater significance than they possess to the things that interest and amuse it. These things conjured up, will perhaps help the reader to take that holiday which circumstances may forbid him.

Contents

List of Illustrations

9

List of Illustrations

Part I
Southern Italy

i

En Route

AS the heel of Italy is approached, the rocky mountains and clamouring vegetation of the spring suddenly flatten themselves out into broad low wisps of land that seem lines of smoke above the water. The latter is more flat, more blue, than anything we have encountered. Here is no sea of graduated and luminous colour, as are those waters that cling so softly to the Sicilian and Neapolitan coasts, but a surface of deep blue, quiet and flat, hard and unyielding as an iron bar.

The grey shapes of the olive-trees, fading into the level, pale coasts, contrast with the cactus and prickly-pear that stand out in menacing staccato attitudes, like sentries guarding their land. The latter, indeed, seem always to be living creatures petrified in some exclamatory gesture. Thus, if through one of man's more brilliant chemical inventions, animal life were to recede from this planet, and the day of the vegetable world was at last to dawn, this plant it would be, surely, which would first thaw into creaking and rather rigid movement.

As man has fortunately not yet progressed so far,

Discursions

the angular and contorted bodies of the Indian figs
are still frozen against the background, their cool
dead colour throwing into relief many blossoms,
burning stretches of yellow broom and small purple
cactus flowers that glow from the ground with a
really Hellish flame. Light blazes with unpre-
cedented vigour on the land, on wave after wave
of vast sea-green cabbages, shaped like full-blown
roses that loll their huge heads, glistening with
dew, close to the ground, while here and there
small white, blindingly white, houses dance through
the heat of the horizon. Flat-roofed, square and
squat as dolls' houses, these are so dazzling that
the cubes of shadow they throw down are more
blue than our bluest skies. On each flat roof is a
small open-air staircase, forming a smaller square
against the backcloth, and looking at first, with its
arrangement of steps, like a Punch-and-Judy booth.

All this wide expanse is sprinkled with towns, the
Greek names of which testify to their former wealth
and power . . . Taranto . . . Otranto . . . Gallipoli
. . . while various small towns and fishing villages
in the neighbourhood still speak a bastard Greek
tongue. Many of the olive-trees, here older and
more fruitful than any in Italy, are stated to be
living relics of Magna Græcia. The country
round, generally, is prosperous and healthy, for the
horrible spectre of malaria, which has made a
desert of Calabria, skulks far away, entrenched in
the marshes of Brindisi, Bari and Metaponto. For

14

In the Heel of Italy

malaria is never met with in a large town, and but rarely in a district as well cultivated as this. Indeed, the anopheles mosquito, like the Georgian poet in England, prefers untended country, with stretches of dank water and an occasional buzzard, where he may brood alone with Nature ; invariably he avoids the city.

Set in these rich surroundings, seven miles from the sea, is Lecce, a city as beautiful, surely, as any that existed here in classic times, however different in its art and aspect. The place itself is a pleasant and gay one with a population of fifty or sixty thousand—a large town for such a district, larger than its neighbours : a clean town, too, with several other peculiarities. The hotel, for example, is one of the few, perhaps the only one, in this part of the world, in which it is possible to stay without suffering. The food is good, and, as in Spain (for Lecce is tinged with Spain), the people believe in " diverting themselves "—which means that they sit up most of the night ; and the cheerful noise of supper-parties resounded through the hotel in the early hours. In the way of amusements, even, and of what, I believe, are known as "amenities," the city has a certain amount to offer—restaurants, public gardens and cafés, for example. The theatrical fare, indeed, seems more varied than is ours in London. On the night of our arrival, Marinetti's band of Futurists were giving their " Surprise Entertainment "—for one night only—

Discursions

in the chief theatre, to be succeeded on the next evening by a Passion Play, and on the subsequent night by a more or less modernised version of *The Dollar Princess*! Then the Municipal Band appears to perform every day, either in the gardens or the chief piazza; and even renders selections from such modern operas as *Boris Godounov* and *Salome*.

The people of the town, simple and unspoilt, unused to foreigners, are friendly to them, showing their amiable intentions by a string of the most charmingly childlike questions—but without any impertinent intention. "You are very tall. How tall are you? Are all your family so tall? Is that your brother? How tall is he? Is your father as tall? How much is his income (is he a farmer?) and how much yours? How do you earn it? What taxes do you pay? Oh! the life is dear, so dear!" These interrogations must be answered affably, though they need not be answered correctly, since imagination should be allowed to enter into the replies as much as it does into the questions.

But chief of all these gentle amusements—there is here a discovery to be made! For the inquiring traveller it is always an interesting study to note at what date the cabs that pass as current were stranded in an Italian—or, as for that, in an English—provincial town. To this day it is possible to find in the North of England cabs that are

16

vast as extinct monsters, and apparently upholstered in their skin. Covered in a crinkly leather, unknown to modern man, but similar to crocodile-skin, only black and soft, and scenting the air within with a vague and rather clandestine breath of oats and beer not altogether unpleasant, these conveyances, fit for the giants of other days, rumble and lumber along station roads: and as the collector will be aware, are known locally as "flies." "Send out for a fly," the provincial lady demands of her maid. Then, at Scarborough, we used to find those very rare little carriages, of an altogether improbable speed and shape, known as "jockey-carts." The drivers of these wore white breeches, jockeys' parti-coloured coats, and rode and drove their ponies — which were usually running away—at the same time.

The blasphemous little postilions, sons of fishermen and with all the lingual resource of their fathers to draw upon, would ride galloping along the roads, by paths of a special asphalt that is like a spotted-dog, past the vacuous prospect of blue bay and jutting headland. Their flaming garments and speed would fit in with the ale-house voices of the nigger minstrels, in striped shirts and black faces, and with the constant warm southern cries of "Hokey-pokey" and the continual jangling sound of bones, clacked and racketed together. The whole scene, of which the jockey-cart was a part, was very pointillist in its effect.

Discursions

It has even been my good fortune to drive through London in a hansom cab balanced on three wheels, the only specimen of its kind in the world, the triumphant invention of its black-bearded and eccentric driver. At all times of the day and night this unique vehicle was surrounded by a gaping though admiring crowd, and its owner carried about with him, and was for ever willing to display, various testimonials from distinguished fares, from eminent statesmen like Mr Joseph Chamberlain or the late Lord Chaplin, congratulating him on his high courage and British enterprise. It was an alluring specimen for the collector, and once enticed towards it, a withdrawal was difficult, since the driver understood humanity, could recognise cowardice, and would not for a moment hesitate to characterise it as such. I was lost. And, as I drove away from Covent Garden in my singular equipage, I must admit to a certain feeling of self-consciousness, increased by the numerous white circles that bordered the pavements, faces gazing up at me under the lamplight. A few days afterwards the war broke out, and the driver was no more to be seen. No doubt in the general rush to make the world safe for democracy, he and his cab, together with many other individual features of European towns—with the jockey-carts at Scarborough, with the tandem and the Bishop-story connected with it, with the Library at Louvain and a thousand other delightful things—have been lost,

In the Heel of Italy

have vanished, or are only retained in the petrifying crystal of our memories, to die when we die.

However, to get on to the grand scale, and forward to the present day, it is not long since I journeyed down to Hampton Court on the last of the road-coaches. Ten-thirty-five at the Hotel Victoria in Northumberland Avenue on Sunday morning, and we were soon "spanking" (for that, I believe, is the correct term) down Pall Mall and St James's Street, a not altogether comfortable journey, for though seated on its moving roof as on a magic carpet, passengers were not, unfortunately, endowed with invisibility, but were, on the contrary, very isolated, very evident, in the rather empty streets, while the slightly self-aware old-roast-beef-tunefulness of the coach-horn clustered together whole bouquets of elderly members, showing like red geraniums, at the club windows. Some of them, I fear, spotted me as "that-affected-young-cub,-dammit,-who-comes-into-the-club-and-never-plays-billiards." Soon, however, we had passed Piccadilly, and were in the more enclosed, friendly spaces of Knightsbridge and Brompton Road. In the glittering glass slabs of the big store windows, stretching on for ever, we could see mirrored the four pawing horses and the elegant shape of the coach, its roof crenellated, castellated with grey top-hats, as if a siege were feared. Faintly through this reflection showed the terrifying spectres of wax ladies in pink evening dresses, in tailor-mades,

Discursions

under large and small hats, mounds of glowing cushions and stacks of farm-yard furniture, rows of mahogany sideboards, mountains of bath-salts, enormous cases of scent and soap, and all the other paraphernalia attached to modern luxury-commerce.

The coach-top, lower than the elevation afforded by the roof of the motor-omnibus, higher, on the other hand, than the seat—or even the roof—of a taxicab, gave us a new plane from which to view the world, another point of view. Everything looked familiar, yet different. The very people in the street were estranged : and the bank manager before whom I had so often sued for mercy, and whom I now saw in top-hat and frock-coat leading his son to church, became transcendentalised and yet more awful—in the Biblical sense.

Then there were the coach enthusiasts. There was the old lady who met the coach in Richmond Park every day, wet or fine, under fierce sunshine, in hail or sleet or snow, waved her handkerchief, kissed her hand to the "whip" and was known as "Mad Alice"; there were the horsey gents who turned up at the posting stations, sucking long straws and talking about horseflesh ; there were the ladies of the inn themselves, hurrying about with refreshments, and, finally, there was the restful rustic idiom of the habituals of the coach— a Doric idiom that, like a cipher, required a key. The coach, indeed, even in its pitiful survival, is no conveyance ; rather it is a dying planet inhabited

In the Heel of Italy

by an almost extinct race of beings, leading their own lives, speaking their own tongue.

France, too, is of interest to the expert. In the provinces was a cab that must have been washed up in that backwater as early as 1830, a cab that was almost a chariot, driven by a coachman whose flowing coat or cape, in three tiers like a pagoda, and language, swept the stranger back to the days of Byron and de Musset, back to the Romantic Age.

And here in Lecce, so far away, so cut off from the rest of Italy, the connoisseur can make a discovery. Usually the cabs of the South are small. At Naples already dwarf, they become smaller as we travel toward Africa; but in this extremity of the peninsula we found a new type, a " Berlino," large as a house, shaky, uncomfortable, but unique—a cab that cannot be opened! To what age do these dusty relics belong, to what does their name refer; to the Siege of Paris, or to some yet earlier catastrophe? Perhaps it is to the Judgment of Paris; but then, where would " Berlin " come in?

Lecce

Few strangers visit Lecce. Even German visitors are scarce, though Gregorovius once delivered himself of the weighty and Baedeker-worshipped observation that " Lecce is the Florence of Rococo art "—a remark that requires some

Discursions

unravelling. From the English tourist, the town seems to have attracted even less attention, though there is an extremely interesting book on Lecce [1] written by the eminent English architect, Mr Martin Briggs.

The chief statements that require making about the city are these—Firstly, Lecce possesses an indigenous architecture, of two periods, which, for the sake of convenience, we can divide into "Baroque" and "Rococo," though absolutely un-connected with these styles as they are to be seen elsewhere in Italy. Secondly, this architecture, a unique flowering caused by favourable local con-ditions, is one of surpassing beauty and distinction. It is this latter fact which needs stating, for, if people are willing to admit the interest of Lecce, they are not so ready to estimate it fully, to compare its loveliness with the beauty of earlier styles elsewhere, to judge it with its peers. If they admit the high quality of its art, then other doctrines must be given up. And the English-man, slow to acquire an idea, is singularly per-sistent in its retention, gripping on to it with his bulldog jaws long after the rest of the world has let go. Indeed, so frightened, still, are many people, even young ones, by the gaunt shadow of Ruskin, that bogey of our nursery, his figure fitfully illumined by the dim religious light of his "Seven Deadly Lamps," that they refuse even to

[1] *In the Heel of Italy*, by Martin Briggs.

LECCE: PIAZZA SANT ORONZA

In the Heel of Italy

consider any manifestation of late Italian Art. They dare not cry, with Aladdin, " New Lamps for Old," and admit that this form of beauty rivals any other to be found in Mediterranean countries.

As to the local conditions we have mentioned, Lecce was in many ways peculiarly fortunate. Always for its size a rich town, it was originally an independent duchy, and even when finally absorbed in the rascally Kingdom of the Two Sicilies, proverbially the most evil rule in Europe, the seat of a perpetual though varying tyranny, was happily too distant from the actual centre of government to have its art-sense crushed for ever. Yet there is no doubt that its development was delayed—but perhaps that partly accounts for the unusually full blossoming in the seventeenth and eighteenth centuries. From the twelfth century onward the city was the centre of a local culture and learning, boasting a literature and school of painting, in addition to its own paramount art.

Another fact which aided the architecture here, was that it passed straight from Byzantine to Baroque, without the intervention of any Gothic-Ingle-nook period. There are, of course, some Gothic buildings in the neighbourhood ; but these are few and appear to have had no influence, never to have become part of the Southern consciousness. Even the various Gothic-revivals have had little success. Throughout the Heel of Italy, Gothic

Discursions

seems to have remained an imported and cold-storage style, hard and frosty. To look its best, this form of architecture must be within reasonable range of the Arctic Circle and Father Christmas; it must be covered with crystal cobwebs of hoar-frost; decked out with traceries of snow and the lingering wheel-like formations of Northern ice. It is true that in Naples there are magnificent Gothic buildings, churches and palaces that are equal to any of their sort in beauty, but these were the creations of French architects brought there by the House of Anjou, and are inappropriate as glacier stones deposited long ago in some Southern valley.

But the enormous advantage that Lecce possesses over all other towns is the great wealth of beautiful stone cropping up to the surface just beyond its walls. And this material is so swiftly quarried, so easily carried to its intended position, that building is always cheap, while the actual softness of the stone when cut allows the rich imagination of the South an unparalleled outlet. It can be carved easily as wood, moulded and modelled, almost like clay, with the fingers; it can be fretted into foam, drawn into a thousand lace-like designs and intricate patterns. Each separate flower in a stone bouquet, burgeoning out of a stone vase, can be cut-out as easily as from paper. Then, after the church or palace is completed, this wonderful stone yields its final gift to man, hardening so that it will outlast our Northern granites.

In colour the stone varies from a tint that is almost white to the richest shade of gold, and out of the latter are most of the important buildings made. If, as in the surrounding villages, white-wash is preferred, the peculiarly flat, even grain of the stone takes it so well that any whited sepulchre is put to shame. Like a semaphore, it flashes a thousand reflections up into the transparent air, and sends enticing little lights, as water does, to dance and flicker like butterflies under the shade of the olive-trees. So pale are the shadows thrown by these white houses that they, too, almost hurt the eyes. The general impression of the country is one of blinding whiteness. Even after dark the houses can be seen many hundreds of yards off, appearing almost luminous, the ghosts of square white cardboard-boxes. And when the full moon sidles up into the blue vault above, the effect, though now faintly tinged with gold, is more than ever overwhelming. The houses seem fashioned from snow, or carved from salt, glittering and cold in the calm night, cooling to the touch. All round are these square white houses, with the white boxes of their outside staircases standing up above them on the roof. Surely, we feel, the lid of the box will soon be forced open from within, and a black-beaked figure in loose shimmering white clothes will shuffle and shamble along the

Discursions

roof, peering down into the blue darkness, and drawing in the cool night air through his mask. For in one of these houses must dwell that figure so lovingly portrayed by artists old and new, by Callot and Tiepolo and Longhi, by Picasso and Severini: here, certainly, must live that curious incarnation of the country, half Italian-Comedy and brigand, half Neapolitan John-Bull, Punchinello!

There were two great periods of building in Lecce, the first from 1540 to 1590, the second from 1660 to 1720, this latter more or less coincident in time with the activities of Wren in England. The second period is perhaps the more interesting, the more perfect expression, and produced two architects of undoubted genius, Zimbalo and his pupil Cino. The break between these two eras of activity was caused by the tyrannical government at Naples, and the consequent insurrections against it such as Masaniello's Revolt. Yet this very retarding process may in the end have forced the flower to a finer growth. The most lovely buildings in the whole town are to be found in the Piazza della Prefettura, where stands the chief church, apart from the Cathedral, that of Santa Croce. It is remarkable how strong is the Byzantine influence, specially noticeable in the sculpture, when one considers that the actual date of its building is about 1580. But then in many of the Greek islands there are altar-screens and episcopal thrones which are purely Byzantine in style, though they were

carved as late as the beginning of the eighteenth
century, and Greece is only fifty miles over the
sea from Lecce. Here, it is true, the Byzantine influence did not linger for so many centuries, for other
traditions sprang up ; but the latter inherited many
things from the earlier style, in the same way that the
Christian religion took over and made use of many
heathen festivals, making them its own. Certainly,
the Byzantine wizardry persists in Santa Croce.
Three large pillars, with capitals of a marvellous
luxuriance, tower up on either side of a fine doorway, flanked by smaller double columns. Kneeling
negro-slaves, lions as fierce as any that crouch in
Africa, yet conventional as a clipped poodle, proud
eagles, boasting golden scales instead of feathers,
winged bulls whose wings are rather short for their
broad foreheads and shoulders, and many other fabulous beasts of great elegance, peer at the stranger
from their ledges. Indeed, so alive are they, in spite
of the conventions of their carving, that the shelves
upon which they stand seem Mappin Terraces.
In a moment we shall see them leap, or hear their
hoarse voices bellowing at us through the sunlight.
The round window above them is framed in a
circular surge, a whirlwind of cupids, tritons, roses
and mermaids, and all that blessed paraphernalia
of the Renaissance, which came to set free the
mind of men again. The hateful age of armour
was over and there came a respite that was to
last for four hundred years, and might, perhaps,

have meant a permanent ending of it. So lovely is the golden colour, so exquisite the workmanship, so complete the unity, that in the whole world there can be few churches more beautiful.

The palace next to it, and adjoining it, is equally lovely and equally elaborate. Begun by Zimbalo in the year 1680, it presents a long façade two storeys in height. The space between the windows is divided by pilasters of cut stone that rise from the ground with an incredible grace. The windows, tapering into strange patterns, are works of a rich fantasy ; each one a separate work of art, yet each essential to the design of the whole building. The themes upon which these fantasies are built up are culled from the common sights of the Leccese country-side. They are drawn from the full, formal curl of the cabbage-leaf, as lovely as any acanthus (and here supposed to be the basic curve of the rococo work, as is the curve of the shell elsewhere), from the swags of flowers that drop in such architectural form under each side of a swelling Spanish balcony, from the wreaths and strings of tomatoes and pimentoes, the clusters of water-melons, grapes, mellowing apples and fissuring pomegranates, that are hung up to dry or ripen beneath the flaming autumn sun. Here in the autumn, as in the vicinity of Naples, whole farm-fronts are covered with such produce, and the effect of the autumn light falling on entire walls of tomatoes and other highly-coloured fruits is indescribable ;

In the Heel of Italy

for the October sunshine seems to have a special aptitude for bringing out every tone of gold and primrose, crimson and purple.

From all these ordinary sights we have described, Zimbalo has wrung out many new, curious and essential patterns, for Zimbalo was a genius as surely as was his contemporary Wren.

The general effect of these two buildings standing together is so new, so extraordinary, that it at first seems the architecture of a new world; and where else, except at Venice, would it be possible to find two adjacent buildings of varying appearance, so different from one another, and yet so harmonious in their whole effect, so sure in their form, so unusual in their decoration, so certain in their mingling of various beauties, that to see them for the first time is like listening to some familiar masterpiece of music, where every note can be followed as it takes up its inevitable place, each a vital part of the whole grand conception?

From the Piazza della Prefettura it is best to walk through the narrow streets full of little open shops like booths—booths in which are hung hundreds of brilliantly-coloured ties to tempt the peasants coming in from the wild regions where there are no shops. Clusters of these ties are hung up outside, like fluttering ribbons, and are the same as the latest patterns offered for sale in Bond Street, only here their price is but a few lira. The open booths are full as flowers of the bee-like voices of the marketers. Soon we reach the Square of Sant' Oronzo. This is the chief chatter-place—and such is a necessity for all Southern towns—in Lecce. Here the prosperous citizens and farmers gather together and talk all day—except from 1 P.M. to 3.30 P.M.—and most of the night. Beneath the pavement of the Piazza lies buried the old Roman theatre, and it is as if all the dead conversations and seething excitements of that place had been woken to fresh life, and have been wafted up to swell the present chorus. The noise, the continual flow of it, is unbelievable. From the many cafés under the Arcade at the back of the Square issues a constant chattering, chaffering, like that of grass-hoppers, mixed with the occasional clanging jangle of mandolins, the hoarse wheezy sympathy of a concertina, or the nasal Oriental singing of a young girl—a singing that bears no relationship to life or music, but is a convention handed on from mother to daughter since the earliest times. Farther on there will be a man, just outside the Arcade, surrounded by a crowd, playing musical glasses ; a trumpet sounds out, another small crowd gathers, and a wildly-gesticulating figure tries to sell cloth at exorbitant prices to the examining, fingering, wary Southerners. And all this din floats up like incense to Sant' Oronzo on his tall pinnacle. Mounted on a fine classical column of sea-green marble, stolen from Brindisi, the colossal bronze effigy of the patron saint, a hand stretched out to bless the conversationalists and itinerant musicians below, entirely dominates the crowd ; a calming influence, one would suspect. In his left hand is a crook, while on it is hung temporarily a large shield-shaped bouquet of paper flowers, placed there apparently by some fanatic steeplejack, for it glitters high in the heavens and the flowers glow very balefully like demons' eyes, arsenic-green, devil-red and wasp-yellow, under the searching light of midday.

Near the base of the column is a fine Gothic loggia, one of the few good buildings of the period in this district.

The town and its suburbs are particularly rich in suppressed monasteries and convents. A little way beyond the town gates stands the ancient church of Santi Nicolo e Cataldo, founded by the Norman (how those Normans got about !) Count Tancred in 1180. Only a portion of the façade is of that date, and is very lovely, though not perhaps more pleasing than the fronts of the later churches in the town. The monastery attached to it is now a hospital. Old infirm men, with a good sprinkling of idiots among them, occupy it, walk down the cool corridors, and tend the flowers. It must be admitted that Lecce is inferior in freaks and idiots to the smaller towns of Spain and Sicily. They are, happily, less visible here. In Toledo, for example—Toledo, which is in any case one of the most frightening cities in Europe, so fleshlessly

Discursions

old and dry, like a skeleton, its bones bathed always in a particularly unreal light (the sunlight more golden, the moonlight more livid than elsewhere) —the general effect is heightened for the stranger at the opening of his visit by the fact that the chief idiot of the town invariably accompanies the hotel omnibus from the station to its terminus. Of a very ape-like cast of face, alternately grinning, grimacing, and biting his arm, he bounds uneasily along, swift but uncertain in his gait. But, indeed, everywhere in Toledo, in back streets and public places, saunter dwarfs, epileptics and cretins. Then at Cefalu in Sicily there is an idiot who carries the same idea even further, for, disguised in a porter's light-blue uniform and with his peaked cap well pulled down over forehead and eyes, he meets the trains and insists upon being useful. A long hand, twice as long as the normal, and with thin simian fingers, is stretched through the open window, and clutches at the visitor's bag up in the rack. He wants to carry the luggage : and it may not be until his face and hands are more fully revealed, or until he gives utterance to that terrible imitative voice, higher than that of a mortal, rising sometimes to a screech, and with no words to it, that the imposture is discovered! Then in the rather wild hills above Amalfi there was the Modigliani-like face of the goose-girl, suddenly thrust forward over a wall, murmuring sweet but toothless nothings through clenched Hapsburg-jaws.

In the Heel of Italy

But here in Lecce the unfortunate, the weak and sickly attend to the cloister garden, where grow masses of lilac and orange-coloured blossom, while green tendrils drift in through the wide arches, spatter the walls opposite with gently-moving shadows, and tap softly against the moss-stained pillars. Over this square of flowers and luxuriant growth, round the well which seems dripping with seaweed, so damp and cool is it on this hot day, stream the fluttering shadows of Judas and Upas trees, their purple and magenta flowers showing leafless against the sky, wringing out of it every ounce of blue transparency. The golden walls are heightened and deepened in their range of tone by the wayward contact of these blowing and growing things, and the Sisters who manage the hospital move slowly and calmly round the cool cloisters and echoing corridors, their vast white head-dresses making them seem ships under full sail. In constant attendance upon suffering, they remain calm and consoling with the quiet, difficult wisdom of a medieval effigy or some remote Oriental Buddha.

Seldom in Italy does one see flowers cultivated to this extent. Perhaps the secret of the successful garden is different from what one had hitherto supposed; perhaps instead of the constant striving to obtain the services of a gardener who is not half an idiot, one should insist at the Registry on being given the real congenital article. But then gardeners are so modest, and would seldom admit the soft impeachment to the lady who sits like a goddess in her office, inscribing such finite words as "sober," "honest" or "hardworking" in her Golden Book.

There is a suppressed convent which is interesting, in the town itself. This is the Rosario, where the monks used to make a famous snuff—that "polvere Leccese" which Napoleon patronised from the beginning of his career until the last day at St Helena. Though the Government have taken it over, snuff is still manufactured here; and since State cigarettes are made here too, it is closely guarded, in case anyone should wish to inquire into the mystery of the substance from which these latter are fashioned. The Church of the Rosario, at the side of the convent, is one of the finest in the city. Within it has the usual numerous altars, with twisted stone pillars, and the almost lace-like patterning of capital and base. The large golden façade has a pediment, supported by pillars, on each side of which are two vast stone vases of fruit and flowers, while two carved peacocks arch their necks and turn them round to peck at melon, pear, and fig.

There is no church, no palace, no piazza, here, but gives some lovely impression; and Lecce is essentially a town of small palaces and piazzas. Of the latter a most charming example is the diminutive Piazza Falconieri, in which are the

two Palmieri palaces, eighteenth-century buildings
full of life and gaiety. The stucco is here tinted
a faint rose, and even the late Victorian face in
bronze, the figure chopped off at the shoulders
and bumped down on a small stone pedestal, while
a symbolic cast-iron palette is allowed to lie negli-
gently at its base, cannot spoil the proportion or
diminish the high spirits of this piazza. The palace
on the right has exquisite rococo windows and
typical Spanish balconies which sail over the
pavement in a ripe curve, obviously intended
to accommodate the swelling crinolines of the
Palmieri ladies. From this vantage-point, as from
a raft anchored high up in the cool night air, they
could watch in comfort the torchlight processions,
the rococo curls of the flames showing up to
advantage their more permanent rivals round door
and window ; from here they could gaze up at the
wavering stars of the fireworks let off on each
Saint's Day, as they powder the dark blue sky
with coloured fire and then suddenly merge into
it ; or sometimes, when music gently washed like
waves at the window, they could peer out through
a mask at the muffled serenaders below. The
other Palmieri palace at the back of the Piazza
is notable for the row of grotesque figures that
juts out from the wall to support the long line of
the balcony. These supports, though they lack the
invention of the ones at Syracuse, or the absolute
perfection of those, described elsewhere, at Noto,

Discursions

where every other detail of a palace is sacrificed
to them, are nevertheless a feature of the town.

Though they are so small, what other name but
that of palace would fit these two buildings? Just
as in England the architect has contrived to disguise
every palace except Blenheim as a house, so here
he managed, without pretentious show, to transform
each dwelling into a palace. And these little houses
are still lived in, still "kept-up." The *cortiles*,
everywhere, are lined with oleanders and palm-
trees in pots, while very varnished cars are being
washed in the water spouted forth by a triton.
For owing to the fertility of the land the Leccese
nobles are still rich for so poor a country, and,
scorning the alien attractions of Rome and Naples,
yet live in Lecce.

Another characteristic of the town is the manner
in which the façades of the later palaces break
into wave-like curves, imparting to the streets an
intentional diversity and grace that must have been
lacking in earlier times. Good building in Lecce,
contrary to our English experience, went on far
into the industrial era; if, indeed, it does not still
continue.

One good building—but here are a thousand—
one touch of imagination, can improve the style
of an entire town, more especially if that town is
not recognised as an art centre. Venice was discovered (though only through the efforts of Ruskin)
to be one of the world's most beautiful cities.

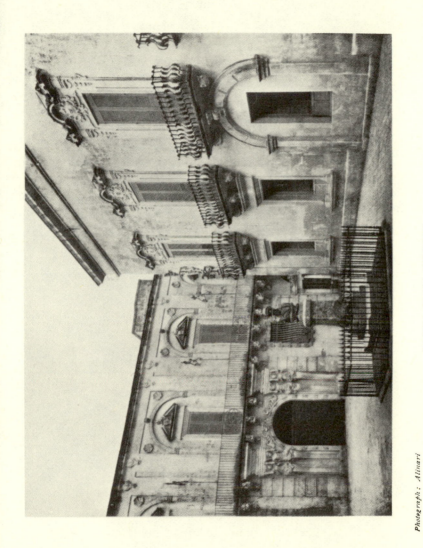

LECCE ; PIAZZA PALMIERI

In the Heel of Italy

Immediately an army of upholsterers invaded it, putting the old capitals of the pillars, washed white with age, salt air, and the constant play of light flashed up on them from the lagoons, into the dark interior of a museum, where they await the Judgment Day in dust and silence. Busier yet, the host of meddlers, not content to deface beauty, proceeds to set up a city of its own, substituting new capitals and columns for the old, slavish cast-iron copies that these men have themselves cut out in their art-studios, converting palaces into newly-mosaiced mansions for the professors, inflicting a thousand subtle little tortures of brick and stone, but mostly of marble, on the unsuspecting corpse of a great city, until its palaces and churches become the model for every club, gas-works and sewage-farm in Northern Europe. Venice is spoilt; and the gas-works lose their chance of a beauty that is engineering.

Brighton, on the other hand, has no reputation as an art-centre, but possesses, quite unsuspected of course by its citizens, one building, not of the highest order, but none the less with a touch of imagination, wild imagination, especially visible in the flamboyance of its interior. This palace has nobly influenced the common architecture of Brighton, and, when the casual visitor, walking along the sea-front, wonders why this arcade is rather more graceful, why this cornice is less hideous, this railing less vile than it would be in

Discursions

London, the answer is—Brighton Pavilion! But the upholsterers have not found this out, though the Pavilion offers them a style nearer to upholstery than those others which they affect. Indeed, the Pavilion contains, much more nearly than Wembley, the seed of a British Empire style. In it, Indian and Arabian art, bamboo staircases made of wrought iron naturalistically painted, pillars of iron that have been turned into palm-trees, huge red and gold lacquer tableaux, honeycomb ceilings, vast chandeliers of gilded wood transformed into flying dragons, Gothic windows and traceries, porcelain figures of life-size holding lamps at the ends of fishing-rods, all mingle together and proclaim, perhaps rather loudly, that the Day of Empire is at Hand! Yet much surely should be forgiven to King George IV., the last of our monarchs to collect pictures or to inspire building on the grand scale, the creator of most of Windsor Castle (and certainly of the romantic effect of it from below, for he heightened and dramatised the Round Tower), of Carlton House, Carlton House Terrace, Regent's Park and Regent Street, the good part of Buckingham Palace, Virginia Water, and the Pavilion. There he would sit beneath a Chinese or Arabian dome, shaped like a cantaloup, refusing to see his ministers, ringing for that perpetual glass of cherry brandy, or occasionally giving orders for the arrest and detention, under the Aliens' Act which he had himself designed, of those horrid

foreign creditors. Two millions, they wanted!
The crowd, which clustered all day round the
Saracen Gate, cheered continually, for, though no
one will ever know why, they loved him. There
he sat, very near his end, all the afternoon and
evening, a little fat man in an auburn wig, with a
fat, creased face, thinking vaguely of the things
that happened in his reign and regency; of that
demented father shut up in Kew, of mad Caroline,
of the daughter who was dead, or pondering on
his problematical part in the great victory of
Waterloo. His poor brain was rather fuddled; it
was so hard to remember. Yet, if after such a life,
he still remained the First Gentleman in Europe,
secure in the affection of his people, what in the
world was there to prevent him from having taken
a great part in that triumph? Just let anyone try
to contradict him! . . . Even the Iron Duke, when
appealed to as a witness of the royal heroism in
battle, had tactfully replied, "So I have heard Your
Majesty say!" And at any rate, he had created
Brighton, in itself no mean victory.

However, to return once more to the sparkling
voices and shrill cries of the South; Lecce has a
thousand beautiful buildings and no reputation.
It has therefore never indulged in the intricacies
of Venetian or Chinese Gothic, or in any variant or
sport of Restaurant-Car architecture. It even dares to
entertain Signor Marinetti, for perhaps it knows what
Venice will learn too late, that Waring-and-Gillow's

and self-conscious-Little-Art-Shops-for-Peasant-Pottery are a greater menace to beauty than all the futurist poets and painters and musicians in the universe. Lecce has never been self-conscious; the lovely florid style of the early eighteenth century refined itself gradually into the simple shepherdess lines of 1760, and then slowly changed into the plainly-built, simple houses of to-day.

The town also possessed a school of painters rather in the Veronese tradition, the last of whom, Oronzo Tiso, died as lately as 1800. In the Picture Gallery are few notable works; but there are some pleasant ones in the Liceo Reale, formerly a Jesuit convent. Here, indeed, is one interesting and delightful picture, though more remarkable for subject than treatment.

In the late seventeenth and early eighteenth centuries, Southern Italy produced a whole horde of miracle-workers and saints. To one of the most extraordinary of these we are introduced by Mr Norman Douglas in his fascinating *Old Calabria*. We refer to San Giuseppe di Copertino, the Flying Monk. This brown-clad brother, who should be the patron saint of all airmen, could fly in at any door or window, without the aid of mechanical contrivances. The secret apparently died with him; but he was canonised.

San Giuseppe was born at Copertino, a few miles from Lecce, and what was our delight to find here in the Liceo, a hitherto unrecorded

In the Heel of Italy

portrait of this extraordinary man, doing a trial-flight, with even perhaps a suspicion of latter-day "stunting"! Clad in his brown habit, the reverend brother is in mid-air, with arms stretched out, high up, inclining, if we may use the term, to a nose-dive, while an elegant assembly of Leccese ladies and gentlemen of the mid-eighteenth century, in white powdered wigs and gay brocades, look on with an expression of mingled interest and polite anxiety.

The other pictures in the building have not the same poignance, but in various churches are frescoes by the Verrio family, which, hailing from Lecce, eventually transferred some of the miracles of the South on to the walls and ceilings of English country houses.

After the Piazza della Prefettura, the finest piazza in the town is that outside the Cathedral, an imposing though not particularly exciting example of sixteenth-century work. The square is an exceedingly large one, full of palaces. The Seminario, the chief building in it, rivals the Prefettura, and is the work of Cino, pupil of Zimbalo, who built it about 1705. Here also is the Archbishop's palace, a delightful arcaded building of the middle of the same century, less rich but equally elegant. The whole square has only one opening, where it tapers to a very graceful gateway opposite the Cathedral façade.

It was our good fortune to see this great square illuminated on the night of Good Friday. In the fanatic atmosphere of Southern Italy the Church dares to move with the times, and a lavish use had been made of electric light. By the side of the Cathedral a large plaster grotto, brilliantly lit, showed the various scenes of Our Lord's life. All the palaces and houses were decorated with lines and garlands of light. Trumpets brayed mournfully in the distance, and from out the dark blue canal of the street floated a procession of strange figures, displayed by the flames of the torches they carried; for the wide square, still empty, though in a few minutes it would become crowded, seemed in the dusk like a stretch of blue water. On came the procession, curling like a dragon, with mournful cries, wailing, and the brazen tongue of a trumpet, while high above were held up the illuminated sacred images and relics. All the figures in the procession were masked, figures from some ballet by Callot, or from a drawing of the Inquisition by Della Bella or Goya. Some were dressed in flowing black with wide black hats, their eyes gleaming through the two slits in the long black cloth that fell over their faces. Some were decked out in light blue and pink—a sort of skirt of blue, and coat of pink—while large red hats, like those of a cardinal, completed the costume; others again wore robes of silver and purple. After them followed an army of children, singing in time to the slow waltz, which by some odd chance had been chosen for the occasion by the Municipal

Band which wound up the whole procession. The children sang in the peculiarly nasal, shrill, meaningless voice of the South. The darkness had increased; it was night. The fixed garlands and festoons of lights now fully displayed the intricacy of the architecture; while the torches, moving through the air, threw distorted shadows on to wall and pavement, gave false value to the stone carving, touched for a moment a door or window, gilded a stone rose or triton, or threw a flickering patch of light like a halo upon some human face. The crowd was now very quiet; and framed by a wandering flood of light in a narrowing swirl of mermaids, roses and cupids, the sullen, bearded face of a monk peered down at the procession, as it slowly filed round the farther corner of the square and out again into the engulfing darkness.

King Bomba

When the flamingo-tinted rays of the early sun lay light as feathers along the ledges and on the sharp angles of church and palace, I was already walking down the empty streets. The Palazzo della Prefettura was still drenched from the night's mists, and the feathers of the sunlight could almost be seen brushing the stone, drying the wet cupids, and wringing the dew out of the huge roses, or striving to rid thicket and mysterious grove of their

Discursions

lingering darkness. The eagles on the church next door were most clearly preening their golden scales, and the lions were shaking their manes free of the dew, while, as if in echo to their deep rasping voices, the folding thunder of shop-shutters, drawn up, sounded out from the main thoroughfares. This was accompanied by continual whistling, sudden floating fragments of Neapolitan song, and the rattle of hurrying feet, though the broad way, in which I stood looking up at the palace, was itself still full of the silence of earlier hours.

The monk's face, set off by the exquisite carving of the Seminario windows, had certainly looked incongruous on the evening before, but it was certain that these much lovelier windows had often served as foil and frame for a yet more unsuitable physiognomy.

Built originally as a convent, this palace had been turned into a royal residence by Murat, and remained such until after the unification of Italy, when it was converted into a museum. For some reason or other it became quite a favourite visiting-place for King Bomba (Ferdinand II.), playing a part in his life, as well as in his death.

In England this king's name is now almost forgotten, or associated only with an excellent Italian shop for the sale of *pasta* and Italian wines in Soho. But in his day he was the terror of his subjects and a spectacle for the whole world. What

44

gives to this monarch his peculiar halo of grotesque horror is the piety, combined with intense cruelty, of all his actions, only equalled by the sanctimoniousness of those who later condemned them, though, whilst he reigned, they never so much as pointed at him a finger. Ferdinand I., Bomba's grandfather, was nearly as much of a monster, but in the frank atmosphere of the eighteenth century, and in the tyrannical air of Naples, so much was freely admitted; nor, though very religious, did he seek to justify every action. But in 1830, when his grandson inherited the throne, the Middle Classes had become masters of Northern Europe; and Naples, though unalterable in its own character, though it remained Greek, Roman, Medieval and eighteenth century at the same time, was superficially affected by the spreading miasma from the North; so that while acting as the traditional tyrant that he was, Bomba° sought to cloak these actions in Sunday garments. This it is that makes of him the most disgusting yet amusing object of his times, for we see him continually after a massacre affecting his "Sunday best," till in this character he acquired an even more perfect technique than his cousin, Louis Philippe.

As we have said, Lecce played a part in his death; and in a guide-book written after Italy became a kingdom—a guide-book which, though it had played the sycophant to him in his lifetime, had become terribly shocked by his reign after it had ended—I find this gloating sentence : " King Ferdinand II. was here (in the Palazzo della Prefettura) seized of a *loathsome* disease, and hurried home to die in *great agony* at his Palace of Caserta."

If the king had recovered and still ruled, the "loathsome disease" would have been transformed into "an interesting illness, unknown to modern science, from which, to the unbounded joy of his devoted subjects, he happily recovered."

In fact, his fatal illness was a most rare one, and has been the subject of several medical treatises. It appears to have been of the same nature as that affliction which laid low King Herod, and does, perhaps, give the final touch of horror to a very gruesome career—a more fitting end even than that which overwhelmed Louis le Bien-Aimé of France.

In the course of a reign of nearly thirty years Bomba often stayed at Lecce. He had many palaces and moved about to a great extent. There was his chief Palace of Caserta, the largest residence in Italy ; then he had a hunting-box at Persano near Eboli, under the knife-like shadow of Monte Alburno. There were the palaces of Formia near Gaeta, and Garditello, of Quisisana at Sorrento, of Portici, and of La Favorita at Portici, another one on Ischia, the Favorita at Palermo, and other residences at Catania and Noto. Yet he found time to stay at Lecce!

Photograph : Alinari   KING BOMBA RETURNING FROM FESTA OF SAN GENNARO

In the Heel of Italy

Fascinating it was to conjure up the fat face of that national misfortune gazing out of the palace, from under cupid-kissed roses and floating wreaths. Here he must have presented a truly superb spectacle, for essentially a royal type, he rather resembled one of the lesser, more despicable Cæsars. The enormous bust, fitted out probably in dark blue uniform, with epaulettes and stiff collar, surmounted by a whiskered face of considerably over life-size, and lacking all expression but one of fatness, must have almost filled up one of these long, lean windows. The people in the square no doubt cheered as he showed to them his vast, unwieldy self. On the other hand they might by then have learned that it was dangerous to greet too warmly any Neapolitan monarch, more especially Bomba. Easily flattered, these kings were yet more easily alarmed. Unusual cheering would make them nervous, while if mixed with it they could distinguish such sounds as the mimic explosion of a blown-out paper bag or a falling walnut, a regiment would spring up suddenly as if from sown dragons' teeth, and before the crowds had stopped cheering some of them would be screaming and the rest for ever silent.

To comprehend the individuality of this most romantic Kingdom of the Two Sicilies, it is perhaps necessary to know a little about both Bomba and his grandfather. No other country in the world except Spain would have tolerated either of them for more than a year or two. But with the exception of Ferdinand I.'s father, Charles III., it is doubtful whether there ever reigned here a wise or kindly ruler. Ferdinand I., however, though not handsome, must have presented a fine appearance —tall, and with a face almost too full of feature, so that he became known among his subjects as "Il Re Nasone," or "Old King Nosey," whereas the grandson lacked even the character of the Bourbon Mask. His was a face altogether impossible to get on to a coin or postage-stamp—and failure in this test should surely disqualify any prince from reigning. Of the two kings, the first Ferdinand had undoubtedly more character, though nearer to lunacy, while the second was more subtly nauseating, though equally cruel. And now that their dynasty is obsolete, and leads a living death, though still bestowing an occasional Order of St Hubert or making public a quite unnecessary, and even rather officious, consent to some royal marriage, the later rulers of Naples present so ludicrous, so fantastic an appearance that it is hard to believe in their very existence. But the family lives on, forgotten, unsought-after even by the crowd of international profiteers who infest the French Riviera every winter—a testimony that such persons as their ancestors lived, that such events took place. And at the actual time of writing there is still a Queen of Naples living in retirement near Munich —that queen whose courage and determination in times of danger were the only redeeming features of the last days of the Bourbons in Naples.[1]

Bomba was as essentially the bad royal type of the nineteenth century as Ludwig II. ("the Mad King") of Bavaria was the good, the former condemning royalty to exactly the same extent that the latter justified it. Of almost undiluted Bourbon and Hapsburg blood for many generations he reflected little credit on these two ancient strains. An exception, to prove this rule of inter-marriage, was to be found in the mother of Charles III., who was the heiress of the Farneses. This race ended in several Dukes of Parma who were remarkable for their obesity; and it is no doubt from them that Bomba drew his full inheritance of adipose tissue. It is unfortunate that no other gift than this should have descended to him from so talented a line.

The chief motives of his reign were religion (and superstition) and family pride, which in him took the form of a belief in the Divine Right of Bourbon and Hapsburg. His grandmother, Maria Carolina, the sister of Marie Antoinette, used to write long letters to the Allied leaders during the revolt of 1799, claiming that Naples and Sicily was "the patrimony of the family." It is extraordinary how

---

[1] Since this was written, Queen Maria Sophia Amalia, last Queen of the Two Sicilies, has died. She passed away on 19th January 1925, at Munich, at the age of eighty-three. Sixty-four years of her life were passed in exile. She was the last Royal personage to be married by proxy.

this view persisted in the Bourbons, and it is related by Nisco that one day in 1844 the old Duke of Sperlinga, a courtier of the ancient type, came to the house of Pasquale Mancini " and told him that he had been present at an ugly scene. The Duke was standing at a window with the King (Bomba) and the little prince to see the people in the palace square crowding round the band at the moment of changing guard; and the little boy asked his father, ' What can the King do with all these people?' to which the monarch replied, ' He has the *right* to have all their heads cut off; but out of respect for our holy religion he refrains from doing it.' And so saying, with his thumb he rubbed the Sign of the Cross on the child's forehead!" In this anecdote both motives of the King's reign are clearly displayed —the Bourbon Right and religion.

Though personally a brave man when danger occurred, the King did not believe in going out to meet it. He was moved by fear of fear, perhaps, more than by danger itself. Unlike his grandfather, whom he resembled in so many other ways, he was not actually a coward if some unexpected danger suddenly occurred, but he did not intend to take any risks. By nature a violent reactionary, he never hesitated to watch the quelling of a revolt from one of the balconies of the Royal Palace at Naples—so long as distance made it safe for him. This condition complied with however, he would stand there like a god, cheering his troops to victory. Behind him, as a background, stretched fifty or sixty years of the most atrocious Bourbon misrule, punctuated by constant rebellions, which, after the royal "order" had been re-established, were followed by the most frightful reprisals on the rebels, and especially on the wealthy middle classes. These reprisals, for the sake of decency, the Court pretended to be the handiwork of the lazzaroni, who were the lowest class of the population, and always to be found ranged on the royal side. It was a convenient assumption, for, once assumed, the lazzaroni were free to wreak such an awful vengeance, such fearful massacres, accompanied by every variant of torture and brutality, upon the King's opponents as not even his Government would dare to inflict. These reprisals would, none the less, be followed by official hangings of any rebels left alive.

Only one thing betrayed the origin of these outbreaks. The troops would be singularly inactive in the protection of the King's quite loyal subjects, for the continual pillage and looting that went on was perhaps an arranged reward for the lazzaroni.

The latter, it must be explained, formed the city-equivalent to that horde of bandits which, lurking in the provinces, also supported the Bourbons. Almost a caste, the lowest population in any European town, this army of forty thousand men, without permanent occupation or dwelling-place, infested the older part of the city, but more especially the Santa Lucia quarter, where the hovels were massed one on the top of another. No one except a member of the fraternity or of the Reigning Family, certainly no policeman, would ever venture to set foot in this vicinity. Like the evil fire within their own mountain, they would remain quiet for years. But on occasions of disorder, mobs of them, dirty and verminous beyond description, dressed in the most terrifying rags, armed with knives, clubs, and guns, would make an appearance in the town to help their King, and, incidentally, to help themselves. When, after the Neapolitan kings were turned out, the Santa Lucia quarter of the town was destroyed and rebuilt, forty skeletons were found under the flooring of one small house alone! In Ferdinand II. they recognised, as they had in Ferdinand I., who habitually spoke their special dialect, their prototype and natural protector. If he went, they would go; for no other Government would for an instant tolerate their existence. Like their kings, they were deeply religious and superstitious, profoundly attached to the Church. Bomba, as did his grandparents before him, if seized with internal pain, would induce a priest to write out a prayer for it on a piece of paper, and would then proceed to masticate and swallow it in the manner of the lazzaroni. Even after his greatest atrocities, if the King were to meet a priest carrying a crucifix

52

or holy relic, he would quickly stop the coach, and, getting out, would grovel before the sacred thing on all-fours, wallowing in the filthy mud or dust of the public roads, unequalled for dirt in all Europe.

Kings Ferdinand I. and II. had a complete realisation of one fact — the only thing, despite the proverb, that the Bourbons had learnt and never forgotten—and this was that in the nature of things all educated people in their dominions must of necessity be their enemies. Bomba believed, as much as ever did his grandfather, or as do now the Bolsheviks, in the theory that educated persons should be kept in their place—which was prison. But unfortunately in his day it had become essential to placate interfering foreigners, English and French visitors who spent money freely in his realm and flattered themselves that they represented foreign opinion. This he attempted by a display of public progress and private virtue. Never, for their benefit, was there a more pious, a more industry-improving, a more family-life-loving monarch than Good King Bomba ; yet this never prevented the Royal Pecksniff from organising a massacre. The Swiss Guard, for example, mutinied, and, after they had been induced to return peaceably to their duties, were suddenly fallen upon and brutally butchered by his other troops. Alas ! Not all these, even, could be depended upon ; and there was one awful moment at a military review in

Discursions

1857 when, as the King went round counting the buttons and comparing the braid with an eye of inherited expertise, a man, named Agesilao Milano, stepped out of the ranks and tried to kill his Majesty, first by shooting and then by prodding him in the stomach with a bayonet. At this moment Bomba decidedly showed courage. Both attempts failed, but consternation was so general that it was some time before the wretch could be arrested.

The man was tried and condemned to death; and though attempted assassination is never a pleasant vice, the method of execution left a little to be desired. It is interesting to know the way in which criminals were executed in Naples as late as 1857, under so progressive a ruler. The following account of Agesilao Milano's death is quoted from Madame Giglioli's interesting volume, *Naples in 1799*, and was given her by an eyewitness. The authoress herself describes this horror of a later day than that about which she is writing, in order to make clear the method in which the prisoners, after the revolt of 1799, were executed by the Royalists. It is the same process that prevailed throughout the eighteenth century. All the political prisoners who were not nobles (and among them several women) died in this way:

"The gallows resembled those in the prints of the last century—a tall upright 'tree,' with one arm from which the sufferer was suspended. To

54

reach this there was a long ladder, and at the execution the hangman, having bound the arms of his prisoner, blindfolded him, adjusted the ropes round his neck, and then preceded him up the ladder, leading the prisoner by the rope, closely followed by the *tirapiedi* (literally, 'pull-feet'), his assistant.

"On arriving near the top, the hangman scrambled up on to the cross-beam, and made fast the rope; then, at a sign from him, the *tirapiedi* suddenly pushed the prisoner off the ladder, adroitly catching him by the feet as he fell, and swinging with him into space. At the same time the hangman from above scrambled down and seated himself astraddle on the shoulders of the victim, and the three swung to and fro in sight of an immense multitude, jamming, struggling and pulling till life was gone."

Needless to say, the lazzaroni immensely enjoyed these diversions; and here is a brief description of what happened after one such execution fifty-seven years earlier.

After the execution, the body (that of a "patriot," or rebel) had been stripped by the hangman, who invariably sold the belongings of his victims. "The body remained hanging naked in sight of the idle crowd. The lazzaroni began insulting the dead body, pushing, pulling, jeering. The fierce game grew upon them: they cut and slashed at it with knives, and finished by leaving nothing

Discursions

hanging but the bones, while they went about the lower quarters of the town carrying the flesh upon the point of their knives. The liver was roasted in the Mercato beside the gallows, and eaten by the vile mob, and a Lazzaro who refused to eat of it was killed by the rest." Such was the gentle populace before whom these executions took place; such the only loyal subjects of the two Ferdinands!

Nevertheless, the royal parade of virtue helped the King greatly with foreign opinion. Twice married, first to a Sardinian, and then to an Austrian princess, he was the father of an enormous family, and during the later years of his reign it was one of the chief wishes of visitors to his dominions, the most sought-after privilege on the part of respectable English tourists, that through the good offices of our minister in Naples they might obtain permission to see the Democratic Monarch drive his family in a wagonette through the gardens of Caserta. The fact that he acted as his own whip greatly endeared him to the sporting English people.

Under the superb marble arches of the Upper Hall at Caserta passes Bomba's immense bulk, suitably decked out for the occasion as an English country gentleman, with just a touch of the professional imparted by his red button-hole, accompanied by his unfortunate well-intentioned queen, Maria Theresa. Behind him marches a perfect "crocodile" of children of all sexes and sizes,

CASERTA : CENTRAL ARCHWAY

In the Heel of Italy

graduated like pearls. Here, out of the enchanted world of the *Almanach de Gotha* step:

Prince François-Marie-Léopold, Prince Royal, Duc de Calabre.

Prince Louis-Marie, Comte de Trani.

Prince Alphonse-Marie-Joseph-Albert, Comte de Caserte (still living).

Princesse Marie-Annonciade-Isabelle-Philomène-Sabazie.

Princesse Marie-Immaculée-Clémentine.

Prince Gaetan-Marie-Frédéric, Comte de Girgenti.

Princesse Marie-des-grâces-Piè.

Prince Pascal-Marie, Comte de Bari, and, finally,

La Princesse Marie-Immaculée-Louise.

Slowly the royal couple, followed by their assortment of Mixed Marys, progress through the geometrical vistas of Vanvitelli's classic staircase, each alley made to look even longer than it is by the false scale imparted to it by this *diminuendo* of children, who, walking in order of precedence, are smaller and smaller in size. At the bottom of the steps the wagonette is waiting. The King is eagerly helped and pushed on to the box, and the rest of the Royal Family are safely installed in it by the royal footmen—the latter the only mortals in the palace whose dress is still in accord with it. Ensconced in this queer vehicle, driven by their monarch, with an English coachman beside him, drawn by two English black horses (there are five hundred English horses in the stables), the Royal

Discursions

Family are soon ascending the broad road which runs right up the hill for three or four miles by the side of the vast water-gardens. Conversation is made impossible for them by the myriad murmuring tongues of the water, but they shout manfully, and Bomba, self-consciously unconscious of prying eyes, often turns round to make a show of family affection, patting and bestowing sweets from a capacious pocket, till tears gleam in the eyes hidden in hedges and woods—for it is felt that if foreigners show themselves, they will miss seeing the genuine affection of the family. This Victorian equipage, these musty nineteenth-century clothes, accord but ill with the landscape created for another age, when it was not necessary for monarchs to pretend to a devotion for democracy. The fountains still flash their feathers up the height of the hill; there are the same level lawns of water, blue and smooth and at a falling angle, on which are cast the bluer shadows of the statues whose frozen gestures are a little thawed by the perpetual soft play of light thrown down on them by the modelling fingers of the sun, and then up again, refined through the transparent depths of water. There are the same falls, brooks, rills, runnels, cascades, and pinnacles of water, turning in the air, dashing a white wing in the direction of the Royal Palace. The marble, still hard as when first quarried, is polished continually by the drumming of falling water, till every vein of colour shows with

In the Heel of Italy

redoubled brilliance, glitters like glass ; and the leaves of the trees are darker and more glossy for the blown moisture. The murmuring voices of the various falls and fountains are the same, for they are faithful always to the songs of their period, and will never sing any others ; but change is in the air, and the dark, dusty clothes of the Royal Family illustrate it. They are not helped, as were their ancestors, by all this display and music. Up the hill they drive to the fountain of Diana and Actæon ; here they get out to look below them at the long façade of the palace, at which are pointed the arrows of all these waters. There it floats in the plain, an immense building, large enough to be a natural feature of the landscape, a mountain, an island, blue in the distance, while over its roof stretches the blue sea, and immediately above it again floats the Greek outline of Capri, like a leviathan, but itself seeming no bigger than the palace. They are now almost too far for English eyes to follow them ; and turning down a side path they enter the famous Giardino Inglese made originally by Queen Maria Carolina, perhaps out of compliment to her inseparable friends, Lady Hamilton and Lord Nelson, and certainly out of reaction from the frigid display of the earlier lay-out. Here they dip into dells of tropical luxuriance, more artificial in their supposed faithfulness to nature than any formal garden, and here, on grass of a truly incredible green, beside huge

Discursions

plants whose variegated leaves resemble venomous Equatorial insects, by a Chinese temple or Gothic pagoda or some other fantastic impossibility, under the fronded attenuated shadow of a tree-fern, the democratic King and his beloved family partake of tea in the English fashion, and can relax into a less demonstrative affection. Yet this kindly family-man-monarch did not shrink from hanging in the palace vast decorative treatments of his subjects being massacred by his soldiers, of burning barricades and all the odious details of street-fighting; though, as far as we can ascertain, these panels were his only acquisitions—the sole clue to his possible patronage of the arts.

This trait appears to have run in the family. After the terrible massacres that marked the end of the first Parthenopean Republic, his grandparents presented Cardinal Ruffo, the victorious leader, with a coffee-set; and on the lid of the box containing it was engraved a pretty and lively scene, the lazzaroni dancing with joy at the royal victory, while eight poor wretches, thin as skeletons and entirely naked, are lined up in a row to be shot. Then, again, since the deposition of the Imperial Austrian House, it has become possible for the tourist to inspect the bedroom, in the Hofburg at Vienna, of the late Emperor Francis Joseph, Bomba's many-times-multiplied cousin, nephew, and royal brother, a monarch much beloved by his people for the simplicity, amounting almost to severity, of his tastes. The palace is a treasury of tapestries, gems, rich marbles, rare furniture, and masterpieces of painting. The State beds are magnificent, suffocating with brocades and plumes. But the Emperor would have none of these. Sometimes he dressed, in the modern royal manner, as an admiral, sometimes as the general-in-chief, sometimes, even, as a fireman. He must remember these professions. His bedchamber was, therefore, a small square apartment, enamelled white, with a small camp-bed in the centre of it ; and on the wall is hung just one picture—a notable painting of the massacre of the Emperor's Hungarian subjects, by his command, in 1848. Such simplicity must have endeared him to all hearts !

King Bomba, in order to placate public opinion abroad, had therefore to cover his more un-enlightened side by an informed interest in such things as sanitation and engineering. Besides, he must please the English visitors, and these were their fetishes. To understand why it should be necessary for him to study the views of foreigners, we must remember that Naples, except in the frequent intervals of disturbance, was from 1780 to 1860 the playground of Europe. One of the largest European cities, it possessed a marvellous climate and unequalled natural beauty. The English well-to-do, before the discovery of the French Riviera by the great Lord Brougham, flocked to it,

Discursions

spending money freely; while the citizens of the
"Paris of the South" (as they prided themselves)
returned the compliment by a craze for everything
English. Ponies, horses, carriages, men's clothes
and boots, food and drink, all must be English.
Everywhere, on all sides, were to be found English shops—grocers and barbers, haberdashers and
shoemakers—while the hotels were resonant in the
morning with hoarse demands (in that baby-language
in which Englishmen address all foreigners) for
eggs-and-bacon.

Quite early in the nineteenth century, while in
England the Regent was still pondering on the
possible illumination of his Pavilion at Brighton by
gas—a new invention—the chief streets of Naples
were already gas-lit. It is true that behind these
broad, well-illuminated thoroughfares, as behind
a screen, lurked, in hovels piled up one on the
other, and entangled with pigs and chickens, every
possible variant of cut-throat, criminal, and cretin,
every species of disease and crime; but to the
foreigner the prospect was picturesque (which is
what appeals especially to the Northern races), and
the favourite promenades were gay and pleasant.
It was all *so* quaint, wasn't it, the huts heaped up
and confused, the steps leading from the lower to
the upper town, right up, it seemed, to the cerulean
sky spread above them? Under the arcade of
San Carlo, the most beautiful and luxurious Opera
House in Europe, the public letter-writers were

62

plying their trade, for only the least fraction of the people could read or write. The crowds moved about swiftly, shrilling like parakeets, finishing the unspoken word with a deft gesture which was in itself speech. The shops were full of cleverly-displayed goods of every description, the tradesmen busy and contented. Highly-varnished barouches, in which elegantly-dressed ladies, drawn by English horses, take the air, jolted along the cobbled streets, mingling with country carts. The women in these wore the multicoloured costume of their districts. The cries of the peasants to their horses as they drive along, cries probably older than any human speech, the cracking of whips and general chatter, the shuddering white lights and blue shadows, the piled-up baskets of flowers for sale, heavy-smelling gardenias and tuberoses, sweet carnations and roses, the stalls of fruit, mounds of figs and grapes hanging overhead in jewelled bunches, the barrel-organs playing airs from the latest opera by Rossini, the constant vistas of little blue waves, the floating outlines of the islands and of the volcano crowned with its tuft of smoke, all combined to give the town an unimaginable animation and colour. Even the mountains here breathed and lived. It was all so unlike London, so quaint! Though the streets smelt "rather unwholesome," it was said that dear King Ferdinand, who loved his subjects as he did his own family, took a great interest in Modern Sanitation—and, of course, in Industry.

Discursions

But that was where foreigners were behind us, wasn't it?

For though the King was already popular with them, he yet made special efforts to propitiate them. He made a show of being modern, of turning his attention away from art toward sanitation and industry. His interest in sanitation was perhaps confined in reality to the construction, at Caserta, of the first water-closet in his dominions. This gay, trellised affair of white and green wood, surmounted by a canopy and decorated with naturalistically-painted branches of ivy, the leaves clinging to the trellis of seat and wall, can still be seen by the inquiring. As for industry, the monarch had caused to be built the first railway in Italy, though it is probable that he considered it more in the nature of a toy than as a method of travel. So enlightened, in fact, was he, that he allowed it to pass in front of his own windows at Caserta, thereby cutting in two the wonderful avenue of plane-trees that, seen from the central archway, continued indefinitely the vista of the cascades. But though anxious to keep up with the times, Bomba, on the advice of the priests, made two stipulations: Firstly, no train was to pass through a tunnel; under a bridge . . . well . . . perhaps; but through a tunnel, no . . . never! For the latter act was held by his spiritual advisers (was it with some divination of latter-day Freudian doctrine?) to be immoral. Secondly, when Vespers sounded, each train must be drawn up at the nearest station, and all non-heretic passengers must get out on to the platform, kneel, and say their prayers. With this object, oratories were hastily erected at each station; though, since these were but small, the majority of those who prayed must still kneel among the milk-cans on the not over-clean platforms. This latter enactment, by providing a spectacle for the tourist on his journey, made the good King more than ever respected by him. Let us picture the scene, for example, at Caserta.

The station huddled close up, under the immense rose and gold palace, is deserted save for a priest in his robes, his small attendants in their white surplices, and a few rather nonchalant but brigand-like porters. The rosy fingers of the autumn sun (for it is an October evening) strum gaily on the thousand windows of the façade, drawing out of them every variation possible. Then the sun flutters them through the leaves of the giant plane-trees on the other side, making a cool murmur, or lets the rich light run through his fingers, trickling down the thick boles. The light is so brilliant that it bestows a certain beauty of texture even upon the porters and the ugly wooden palings that border the railway-lines, while the white robe of priest and acolyte are turned into rich velvet. Peering out behind you at the palace, you cannot see the royal face at the window, for the larger, more fiery, circle of the sun strikes back at you, but through the central archway you can still detect a former age, a long white-thread-like vista of arches, trees, and snow which you are aware is running water. For though the great cascade dashes down in foam and spray with a noise like galloping centaurs, so distant is it at the end of the vista that you cannot detect the flashing movement of it, but only the whiteness of its leaping waters, till it seems a glacier or frozen avalanche. The formal avenues and plantations become black marks—semicolons and full stops—a punctuation that conveys nothing to those ignorant of the language of this garden. The rosy light becomes paler, the sky comes nearer and more blue, while into it, above the intense crimson of the sunset, radiating through ugly ochreous layers into this tone of blue, one primrose star flutters out like a bird. Now the first Angelus threatens from the distance, and soon the air quivers and becomes fiery with all their brazen tongues, those little flames of sound that, fanned by the evening breeze, lick the mysterious impregnable walls of silence in garden, avenue, and wood. Far away, above the avenue, shows the red glow of the volcano, and as if in answer to its call, another red glow appears on the right. This equivalent flame is that of the train, which has been slowing down for some time, and, it must be said, without much difficulty. It now rackets and bumps and wheezes into the station; the small engine has a funnel made, perhaps out of compliment to foreigners, in the image of a top-hat placed upside down. The priest watches fretfully; but now the doors are flung open, and a hurrying crowd of gesticulating, dark little men and women precipitates itself upon the platform; the women, in black mantillas, dart toward the oratory, the men kneel on the platform, while the more tall, angular shadows of the foreign visitors look on. Crinolines, whiskers, and pipes are lost in the darkness, and the large shape of the hat, which is wanted to complete the grotesque male silhouette, is lacking; for the hats are in boxes on the rack, while their owners have adopted for the journey soft check caps. Some of the groups watching are pleased at the piety, others shocked at the idolatrous superstition, which such a service indicates. "See Naples and die" they hiss to one another in voices louder than they ought to be; now they reduce their tone a little till it mingles with the soft broken murmur of prayer and response, until gradually the little waves of darkness blur their outlines, blot them out, each wave as it sweeps silently in making them less distinct, as each wash of the tide diminishes a sand castle. Finally nothing is left on the platform but the prayer, the answer, and the sibilant voices of the North.

In later years the King and his spiritual advisers withdrew their objection to tunnels as such; and it is with great pleasure that I am enabled, through

Discursions

the courtesy of the director of the Museum at San Martino, to reproduce, for the benefit of my readers, a lithograph of the opening of the first railway tunnel in the Kingdom of the Two Sicilies. The original hangs in the Bourbon room in the Museum at San Martino. It is a pretty scene: above the steep escarpment, and below, stand grenadiers, very wooden on the hill-side. The seething crowds, excited by such an event, press in between the troops, who, in the act of presenting arms, are thus unable to interfere. Above the specially-constructed chapel in the foreground banners flutter proudly on the blue Mediterranean breeze. At the moment the bishop's arms are outspread in blessing and exhortation. Flounced crinolines, draped and sloping shoulders, and flat, circular little parasols tremble with excitement. Even the stronger sex is not altogether unmoved as the royal band gurgles a serpentine salute down the coils of its brazen instruments, for in a second the Royal Train will appear, issuing out of the First Tunnel in the Realm!

Another reproduction which I owe to the courtesy of the same director shows King Ferdinand and all his august house on their way home, after witnessing the annual, indeed perennial, miracle of the liquefaction of San Gennaro's blood. In the foreground are the usual English families, disguising their admiration for the King under the assumed indifference that befits a race of conquerors. The paterfamilias is crowned with the inevitable funnel-shaped hat,

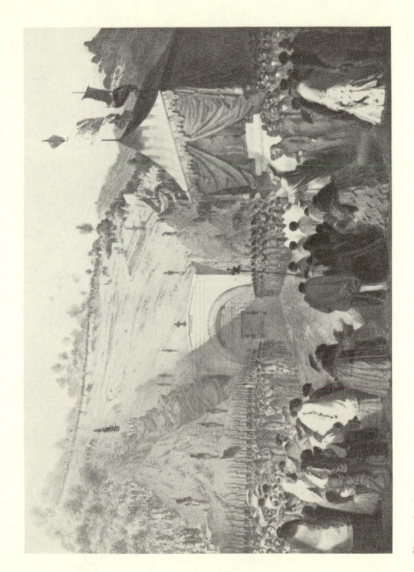

Photograph : Alinari

NAPLES : OPENING OF THE FIRST RAILWAY TUNNEL.

In the Heel of Italy

which to this day has left so deep an impression on the popular memory in South Italy. The mother, every inch a matron, stands very upright and calm, her crinoline giving her an added dignity, while another of those flat, circular little parasols, like a penny, guards her complexion from the rays of an alien sun. The children are excited and stamping, dancing indeed, in long frilly trousers and little Persian skirts above the knee, or else in variations upon tartan and kilted themes. The procession draws near them, and they are suddenly quiet, frozen in their attitudes of impatience. First come the running guards, clad in plumed caps, tunics, and white tights. They brush away imaginary obstacles to the royal progress. Hard on their heels follow six English royal horses—white horses—each, as if a debutante at its native court, supporting on the top of the head three ghostly, nodding plumes. These gallant animals paw the ground in a rich curve as they bear along the royal coach. In the nearest window shows, like a slightly-whiskered full moon, the immense round pallor of King Bomba's face, while beside him a rather wistful consort shrinks into the farther corner. Behind the coach is that delightful Spanish arch, built of lava and stone, and usually covered with flowering snapdragons, above which stands a green bronze saint with a halo similar to a Red Indian headdress. But the coach is in the open piazza now, driving through the sunlight, only broken at frequent and regular intervals by the absurdly-elongated phantoms of the Thirty-Four Virtues of Charles III.—for such are the immense stone figures which cast these shadows. Posturing high up in the blue air, they testify to the unworthiness of Charles's great-grandson who drives beneath. Probably, however, at the time of this progress, a presumption of less than thirty-four virtues for any Neapolitan Bourbon would have amounted to *lèse-majesté*. This number was merely a form of royal salute, a compliment, like the decree of so many cannon-shots to an Indian Rajah. All the Bourbons would, no doubt, take precedence by the number of virtues officially assigned to them, and these salutes were probably based on a chart drawn out by the Sun King himself!

A pilaster rises to sustain the weight of each virtue, and between each two pilasters are slung up two balconies and, beneath them, a shop. Even the balconies are crowded, but this time, I think, with Neapolitans, for about them is a more flashy elegance, a suggestion of Africa; the whiskers are blacker and more pronounced, the crinolines are more exaggerated, the waistcoats more waisted.

But for our nation this picture has a special interest. That slight, wistful figure at the back of the royal coach might have been such another, more familiar—one that was in time to gather substance. For it is said that, between his marriages,

In the Heel of Italy

King Bomba was suitor for the then fragile hand of the Princess Victoria of England. Alas, there were religious difficulties! What developments would there have been? Would Bomba have been transformed into Ferdinand the Good; and would Victoria, instead of becoming, as Mr Kipling calls her in one of his best poems, "The Widder o' Windsor," have become translated instead into " La Vedova Catolica ma Inconsolabile di Caserta"?

There were to be no such flowerings of the imagination. Bomba espoused his Austrian, and it was from this lovely Palace of Lecce that he "hurried home to die in great agony."

His son, that poor ghost of a king, reigned but a year : then, after the fall of the Bourbons, the guide-books discovered what an unpleasant monarch their favourite had been, and the order of St Hubert is now distributed in the more obscure purlieus of Cannes.

Puglia

Our party attracted a certain amount of attention, consisting as it did of a negro chauffeur, the two very large proprietors of the garage, each carrying a bottle, strictly in scale, of Malvasia di Lecce—a delicious local wine—and ourselves. The negro spoke good English and better Italian. Asked, perhaps tactlessly, if his home was in the West Indies, he answered, with the cold pride of an

71

Discursions

Imperial race, " I am Portuguese "—though when subsequently greeted as Our Oldest Ally, he was somewhat mollified. Unfortunately his European origin was not made obvious in the cast or colour of his countenance, and, as we were whirled through the streets of town and village, small children with blending memories of Verdi's *Otello*, the Saracen invasions and those corsairs that were so dreaded only a century ago, cried enthusiastically, " Il Moro ! " or, more affectionately, its diminutive, " Moretto ! " The Portuguese gave no sign of hearing these innuendoes, but drove on, wrapped in a mantle of sable dignity that seemed more Spanish than Lusitanian.

Out of courtesy, and perhaps a little curiosity, the two proprietors of the garage had decided to accompany us. No Englishman appeared to have visited Lecce since the war. None had ever (no, never within memory !) visited Gallipoli, except a few on war-duty. Certainly no one had ever driven there for pleasure. Where was the traditional and expected top - hat of our countrymen, symbol of Empire ? Why go to Gallipoli ? Questions such as these had evidently been well discussed in the past twenty-four hours, if, indeed, they had not formed the excuse for an informal party on the previous evening—this we deduced from a lingering though rather weary joviality in the manner of the two owners, and from occasional remarks on the part of their many fat friends, who, even at this early hour, came to give them a send-off. The final and general conclusion was that we were bound for Gallipoli, because we were afflicted with a liking—amounting almost to a morbid passion—for *zuppa di pesce*, here euphemistic for "boiled cuttle-fish," a speciality of the surrounding coast.

As we glided swiftly past the golden façades of church after church, palace after palace, it seemed in the swimming light of the early morning as if we rode down an endless avenue of twisted stone columns, pompous bouquets of stone flowers, elongated statues, and cherubs blaring a soundless song of Resurrection from their long trumpets up into the sparkling air—an avenue as fantastic as Piranesi's Appian Way, a street from some city in another planet. Soon, however, we were arrested by a misadventure. Malvasia di Lecce is a sparkling white wine; and one of the bottles, the stoppers of which were fastened down with string, suddenly drove out its cork with an immense noise, as of a mine being exploded, while a torrent of sparkling liquid splashed in a golden fountain over a passing lorry. It was like the launching of a battleship; the hubbub was indescribable. Gesture and speech vied with one another in intensity of expression. Eventually the affair was smoothed over, and we were soon safely on the outskirts of the town.

Here the houses thinned out, becoming more simple, until they ended in a suburban flourish of

Discursions

German New-Art (1898-1908).   One house indeed
was particularly noticeable.   Its doors were shaped
like horseshoes, as were the windows, but the
latter were filled with that heraldic stained-glass
associated with the parlours of English Dentistry,
while the walls of the whole edifice were decorated
with such emblems as scrolls of music, conductors'
batons, crotchets and Æolian harps—the house, we
presumed, of some retired local Prima Donna.

The country now asserted itself with stretches of
flaming yellow broom—for the rest, everything is
white or grey.   A level land it is ; old riven olive-
trees, white houses, fruit-trees, and the flat yet
fleshy shapes of the various cactuses being the only
vertical objects in it.   Houses, walls, roofs, fences,
roads—all are white, while even the lime-washed
trunks of the fruit-trees seem more dazzling than
those in English orchards.   The trees themselves
are in full blossom, sailing like low clouds over
the gardens ; each one is a snowy nimbus anchored
there, for there are no other than these to stand
out against the intense blue of the sky.   The lines
of shadow between the rows of fruit-trees, as one
looks down them from the road, are long white
tunnels formed by the blossom above, the trunks
at the side, and the petalled ground beneath, till
the whole landscape seems to be melting under a
load of snow, very scintillating, and containing
within it under the fierce light all the colours of
the spectrum, yet sent down to temper the warm

morning air. All these different white surfaces—the planes of the house-walls, like mirrors, the uncertain lines of the blossom-drifts, the convex and concave of the tunnels—throw watery reflections into any lingering patch of shade. This intense whiteness alternates with tracts of grey merging into blue-green; pallid rocks crop up to the flat surface stained with moss and lichen, olive-trees stand in gnarled rows, for hedges there are cactuses and Indian figs, while filling up the furrows of the ground, uncurling themselves for ever into the distance, are the full-blown forms of the cabbages, still jewelled with dew: then again long white tunnels, full of the honeyed scent of fruit-blossom.

Though the villages through which we passed appeared quite empty as we approached and entered them, yet we had only to pull-up the car for an instant to find it besieged by a crowd of children, all panting and crying " Il Moro," while they again were encircled by a taller band of inquisitive but more silent elders. The villages are numerous and surprisingly clean. The farms that stand alone in the country, the houses in the environs of the village, are whitewashed; but the chief buildings everywhere are built in the same style, and of the same gold or fawn stone that makes the colour of Lecce so beautiful. Copertino, Soleto, San Cesario, Galatina, Galatone, Nardo — all are built in the Leccese manner, which gives to this imaginative race such full and individual vent. Set in the

country, too, these churches and palaces look so
much a part of it, that surely no other form of architecture would be thus suited to its environment.
Each village has churches that are wonderful, the
chief ones usually being sixteenth or seventeenth
century in date, while the palaces mostly belong to
the late seventeenth or the eighteenth century, here
—as, indeed, everywhere else—the great period for
domestic architecture. The latter, though small in
scale, are usually very fine in planning and detail,
having the inner court and staircase, the masks
and Spanish balconies that are so delightful a
feature of houses throughout the province.

In spite of these numerous small palaces in town
and village, there appears to be only one country
house, as we in England understand it, in the
whole foot of Italy. This remarkable edifice was
built at the beginning of the seventeenth century
(though there are traces of the original feudal
castle), and it is situated at San Cesario, near
Cavallino, about four miles from Lecce; but, alas!
it is now more or less ruined. It belonged to the
Duke of Castromediano, whose family was formerly
the richest and most powerful in all the district.
The late Duke, last male heir of his family, was
the famous "Patriot-Duke," and seldom can an
ancient and honourable race have ended in so noble
a flourish. It was the perfect end, if there had to
be one, for such a family of warriors and statesmen.
All his life, till he was almost an old man, he

spent in a heroic fight against the tyranny of the
Bourbon despotism in Southern Italy. Though
offered every bribe and honour by the King if he
would hold his peace, he persevered and fought
on. Most of his early manhood was spent in the
Calabrian and Puglian prisons, the conditions of
which in the early nineteenth century were quite indescribable. The foul air was reeking with typhoid
and malaria; the prison authorities kept to themselves any food or clothing that came in their
direction. Nothing sent to a prisoner ever reached
him. Insufferably hot in summer, the winter was
even more of a torture, for half naked, and with
scarcely any food to warm himself, the prisoner
must pass his time in a cell which was often half
full of water. Most prisoners, unless they were
peculiarly hardy brigands (but under the Bourbons
the latter seldom saw the inside of a prison), lost
all hope and determination, and never more appeared in the outside world. But the Patriot-Duke
escaped time after time, and was the rallying-point
of the fight for Italian freedom in the South. Yet
often he was left to fight alone. His estates were
forfeited, his followers forgot him.

The eventual triumph of Garibaldi in the district
was largely due to Castromediano; but when the
unification of Italy was completed, the family
estates were never restored to him, and he was
too proud to make constant application for them.
The admiring citizens of Lecce made him their

Discursions

Public Librarian, but the salary which at that time they could afford to give him was only just enough to enable him to exist. His house was still left in his possession, and there he lived, in great poverty in one room, never grumbling. And there, only a few years ago, he died at a great age; and the house has passed to a nephew, the son of his sister.

It is a very large one of three storeys; the façade, which, though handsome, is not in the same category as those at Lecce, has a fine doorway with two fluted columns on each side and a balcony above. In recesses between the windows on the first floor are statues, some of which are antique, others of the same period as the house. Over the centre and largest window is a vast coat-of-arms, and above each window in this storey are busts in circular niches.

The actual vaulting of the doorway which leads to the courtyard shows traces of the older castle, of Gothic workmanship; while through it you are confronted with an enormous stone statue of a man in armour, a statue twice or three times life-size, an impressive and hieratic work of art. It stands there like a family god, against a background of ancient broken walls, under the mysterious shadow of tall trees and clinging branches, whilst all round it the old palace, which it seems to typify, crumbles into golden dust. With one hand the statue points to the great hall on its left, a vast room, the outside walls of which are undoubtedly Gothic, though, through the unglazed windows, we could see a painted ceiling of a later date, and, on the wall, the gigantic figure of a Roman emperor in kilts, directing his forces. The gilded trophies that shine from between the panels are already decaying, and will soon have disappeared; even the solid stone is dissolving. The entire building, except for the façade, is in a semi-ruined condition; but the imposing staircase still stands there, with many armorial bearings above it and inscriptions that celebrate the various visits of Spanish viceroys or of the earlier kings of Naples.

Only a few years ago there was still in existence a large formal garden attached to the house, the only one in all this part of Italy. Presumably it was as different from other formal gardens as the palaces in Lecce are unlike other palaces; but there is no record of it left; and now it has been destroyed, to make way for a most hideous *Giardino Inglese*, a subtropical horror of dwarf palm-trees, footprints in the dust, and red geraniums. Even in England it is barely forty years since the formal garden emerged from under the cloud that had covered it for a century and a half. In Northern Italy it has only half emerged, while here, where everything is so belated, the cloud is only just appearing, and the many minor Capability-Browns and Wyatts of Lecce and Taranto are now on the very threshold of their careers! It is, then, not possible to find out from them what the old

garden looked like, while the only Englishman
I know who, had he wished it, was competent to
describe such an oasis, has the misfortune to be
elderly, and to disapprove of anything later than
the first Black Death, upon which all his calcula-
tions are founded. This gentleman was therefore
content to say, with an air of great disparagement,
that "it is the sort of thing you young people
would like," and then proceeded to a fatuous comparison of it with cubist pictures. Alas, if only it
were true! . . .

The other palaces in the villages are not country
houses, but miniature town ones. The best of
these usually belong to the Bishops, for, except in
Lecce, where there is considerable secular wealth,
it is in the churches, and in the palaces and
monasteries attached to them, that the accumulated
treasure of the community is to be found.

Though the prevailing effect of town and village
is of the Baroque period—not the usual Baroque, but
a fully-developed indigenous style—the churches
generally have traces of earlier work, and in each
of these villages there is at least one small church
entirely decorated with frescoes of the twelfth,
thirteenth, or fourteenth century. Unfortunately,
though the later buildings have been left alone,
these decorations have almost invariably been re-
touched. Restoration, which, even when well done,
inevitably kills the soul of the thing restored,
is in this district grotesque beyond words, the

In the Heel of Italy

fruit, probably, of a happy co-operation between
the village carpenter and local ice-cream manufacturer. Where, however, it is possible to see
what the original artists intended, the feeling of
the early painting, even allowing for the very
strong and lingering Byzantine traditions, seems
more Greek than Italian : and since Greece is so
little distant, it is not improbable that these frescoes were actually executed by provincial Greek
artists, perhaps disturbed in their homes by rumours
of the gradually advancing hordes of the Crescent.

Certainly, though, the tradition lingers in this
extremity of Italy, and it is often difficult to be
sure of the actual date of such things. Thus in
a church in Gallipoli (a town which, unlike Lecce,
developed no very definite architecture of its
own to supersede the earlier styles) we discovered
a fresco, absolutely Byzantine in feeling, which
represented the martyrdom of about twenty early
Christians. Many severed heads lie about on the
ground, like flowers with red stalks, wearing a
piteous but quite conventional expression. One
man is just having his head removed by a crescent-
shaped sword, while the headless trunk of yet
another martyr is being displayed to an affable
and condescending emperor. The latter is sitting
cross-legged beneath an Oriental canopy, his head
bowed beneath a turban as enormous as that of
the Grand Turk himself. Although this fresco is
so primitive in style, most of the bodyguard and

F   81

all the martyrs are dressed in mid-sixteenth-century clothes. It must, therefore, have been painted after the destruction of Otranto by the Turks under Achmet Pasha, Grand Vizier to the Sultan Mahomed II., in the summer of 1480. Of Otranto's population, which was estimated at twenty thousand, twelve thousand were massacred in circumstances of the utmost horror, while the remaining eight thousand were carried away and sold as slaves. Not a soul was left out of this peaceful and prosperous community, and it is little wonder that the town never recovered from the blow. A profound effect must have been created upon the popular imagination by this event, and we think this influence was to be felt in the fresco before us. For several centuries, doubtless, after the sack and massacre of Otranto, the earlier oppressors of the Christian faith and their victims would be visualised in this neighbourhood in the later, more actual terms of Turk and Infidel; the memory of it would linger like a nightmare at the back of the mind for many a generation.

It was on our way to Soleto that we noticed an ancient church, slowly sinking into the flatness of the shrill, yellow-green cornfields of the spring, untended apparently, and with only a few black cypresses standing near the door, like exclamation marks, to attract the attention. We drove up to examine the façade. Near by, under its very shadow, was a small cottage painted in pink and

In the Heel of Italy

white sugar-stick stripes, and out of this presently emerged the custodian of the church, a real tortoise of a man, slow, decrepit, cautious. Dressed in his official uniform, he crept along by the railings, clutching a key larger than himself, a fine old iron key. The Moretto now displayed a cruel and barbarous sense of humour out of keeping with his character of a Portuguese (or, as our fathers said, a " Portingal "), a race notoriously kind. " Hullo, Father!" he cried, gurgling with Lusitanian laughter, "what a time you've been! And now, don't you recognise me, your youngest and most devoted son?" The old man looked up at him with that vague tragic gaze of senility, to which nothing is impossible. The eyes tried with infinite care to focus, to pin down the fact in front of them, as though it were a moth or butterfly to be set-out. For a long time he studied in this manner the dusky grinning physiognomy before him—for so long that the joke began to grow cold, to stiffen in its joints, and become painful, even to Il Moro— and then replied in a quavering voice that contained no trace of irony, " No, figluolo mio, I should not have known you. You have grown so dark." Yet he did not seem surprised when his son left him again after so short a time! A queer life it must be, to live unattended, between the ages of eighty and ninety, beside a derelict church in green deserted fields, with no memory of the past and no hope for the future.

Discursions

Soleto has a fine cathedral, with a campanile that must be one of the most beautiful south of Naples. Built early in the sixteenth century and Gothic in style, it yet seems to be a spontaneous and natural growth, for it has in it all the elements and fantasy of the later architecture. The tower rises three storeys above the church; the two lower ones are square. Each side has a Gothic window of great elegance—a *bifora*—divided in half by a slender twisted pillar. The top storey is hexagonal in shape, with smaller windows of great richness, and above it is a cupola of coloured tiles. The jutting-out cornice of the first storey has standing on each of its four angles a very unusual gargoyle that suggests a Chinese grotesque of an early period rather than a piece of medieval sculpture.

From the top of the campanile a wonderful view is obtained. As we ascend the stairs, at each window the real rhythm of the country becomes more perceptible, a rhythm of surface more than of shape, and therefore more difficult to realise except from a height. As we get to the top of the tower, the innumerable white houses below fold up suddenly like so many gibus-hats, and at the same time the flat-chested elegance of the prickly-pear-trees, which so largely dominate the landscape below, disappears and is lost. Instead of these things is an abstract pattern in lines and dots of grey, brown, white and blue, stretching on for ever. The cabbage-fields are brown and grey, the fruit-

SOLETO: CATHEDRAL TOWER

trees are white dots, while the olive-trees seem to
interpose a smear of grey smoke between the landscape and the beholder. On and on the flat land
stretches, till it ends in a sudden border of hard
blue sea, barely separated from the sky.

The windows of the church itself are of a later
date, and have stone grilles instead of glass. These
create an impression of great richness; the colour
of the stone is golden, and through the spaces
shows the sky that flowers like a gentian. The
whole building, indeed, evokes the Jesuit churches
of South America more than any Italian one, for
these windows are rarely met with in Europe.

The cathedral contains many interesting objects;
among others, a curious Gothic wooden pulpit,
carved early in the fifteenth century. The base of
this structure is supported by six carved crocodiles
—an eccentric support never to be encountered
elsewhere. The heads of these creatures betray a
strong African influence, having the same rather
horrible delicacy that belongs to the ivory fetishes
of the Congo valley. What could Puglian workmen
know of this Equatorial monster? St George,
it is true, is often represented in the act of killing
a crocodile, but seldom in Western Europe. The
St George in Venice probably came from the East.
On the other hand the crocodile was much prized
in the alchemy of the Middle Ages, and it is possible
that some wealthy local alchemist, in his perpetual
but fruitless search for the Philosopher's Stone,

may have had one of these reptiles imported from the opposite continent. Or is it merely that the wicked, nerve-racking south wind brought across with it the primitive feeling of African forest and river-bed to this ancient civilised land?

Yet, though the crocodile is still happily a rare phenomenon, this latitude is the playground of an equally venomous creature, the tarantula. The bite of this giant spider is in most cases fatal; but, in addition, the legend grew up that it was responsible for the peculiar dancing madness which was at one time of such frequent occurrence in South Italy. From the name of this spider, and the legend attached to it, developed the national dance the "Tarantella." The queer logical sequence behind this folk-dance was, I think, the idea that since a man after he had been bitten (so it was believed) danced furiously, he might, by dancing furiously, avoid being bitten!

Outbreaks of this dance-mania occurred quite late in the nineteenth century, but unfortunately were never scientifically observed. The person first afflicted usually gyrates on until he or she dies of heart failure, and often the infection spread until half the village had joined in the fatal dance. An old friend of the writer's has described to him how, passing through an out-of-the-way village in Calabria some twenty-five years ago, he saw a woman whirling round madly in the piazza, surrounded by a crowd. The onlookers told him that she had been bitten by a tarantula and had already been dancing for twenty-four hours. Unfortunately the traveller did not stop to see the end of it. This madness, perhaps a form of epidemic hysteria, was also fairly common in Greece, and may be related to the gyrations of the dancing dervishes. A party of courageous psychoanalysts should be ready equipped for the next outbreak.

To get back to our crocodiles, it is certainly an odd thing to find their effigies in this lovely old church. They would be more in keeping with the rites of worship in some temple, on the slimy banks of a jungle river; and the pulpit has an unpleasant air about it—too sirocco, too tropical.

The country became, if possible, even flatter as we neared Gallipoli; and the hard blue ribbons of the sea fluttered again on the horizon. Gallipoli itself is on an island and presents the appearance of a small fortress-like rock, crammed with gaily-painted houses; it floats like a parti-coloured banner over the prevailing flatness of sea and land. It is, though smaller and not so beautiful, not altogether unlike Syracuse; but it is impossible to imagine how the population of ten thousand persons is compressed into so restricted a space. A wide bridge-road connects the town with the mainland, on each side of which is the sea, so hard and blue in the distance, but clear as green crystal when one looks down into its waters. At one side of the bridge is an interesting Roman fountain, a large and well-preserved affair, with a fine bas-relief set into the back of it. The town was important in Greek and Roman times, and rich, as it is now, from the great quantity and excellence of its wine and oil. These were stored, as they are yet, in vast caves and cellars in the rock, hewn out, like the Latomia at Syracuse, in pre-Greek times by some unknown race.

The Portuguese and the two garage proprietors, carrying the one remaining bottle of Malvasia, hurried out of the car. We were rather late, and there might be no cuttle-fish left. We walked round the town, a town in which the palaces are more interesting than the churches, rather un-inspiring after those we had lately seen. The narrow crooked little streets are full of palaces, built here of a grey stone which lacks the rich-ness of colour that makes Lecce and its villages so lovely. The palaces, though quite different in style, are of the same period as those at Lecce, and are large and well designed. But every street, except the few main ones, ends in a sudden, un-expected cul-de-sac of blue sea; for the streets are not straight, and the vista appears only toward the ends of them. Wandering through the crooked alleys, we heard a mournful wailing, and at an un-expected twist of the road came upon two figures clad in black Inquisitorial garb, their eyes peering at us through the mask of the high-peaked cap. So much in keeping they seemed with the old

In the Heel of Italy

town, that it was some seconds before we were even surprised by their appearance. Now all the bells of the churches began tolling, their voices deep or cracked, till the air was full of warning utterance. Some of them would suddenly beat fast and madly, as the heart beats out at a sudden fright, while others would mourn steadily in their bass voices; nor did the surrounding expanse of sea in any way muffle the brazen din, for the tongues of the bells, as their mourning grew louder, seemed to catch in the hard stonework of the houses, high up at the cornice, and round the windows. It seemed as if they were shouting in at the upper windows, warning even those who might be seeking rest from the fierce rays of the midday sun. "Get up! Get up! Get up!" they repeated, at each fresh swing. The reverberations sank down again from the upper air, and could almost be heard striking the hard cobbles of the streets. There was as much sound in each street as there is water in a canal, so that each man standing there was soaked through with it, drowned with it. The whole town was inundated, as if the blue water had upreared itself into a venomous wall, and all the houses were sinking beneath the fierce rush and swirling eddies. Still the bells tolled out, on and on, and under the brilliant trembling light, such light as belongs only to Southern waters, figures in the strangest dresses were collecting together or marching along in little

bands. The first figures were all those of In-
quisitors; but these were soon followed up by
others in red and blue, or in scarlet and purple,
with wide hats or peaked caps. These garments
had nothing of fancy dress about them, as they
would have in any procession of their kind in
England or France. Here in their appropriate
setting, in the narrow streets, with the gloom of
wide, cool courtyards behind them, under the
fullest midday light, which showed a hundred
shades of colour where before there had been but
one, they carried the onlooker not so much back
to any historic period as to some undiscovered
land and unknown civilisation, to Mexico under
Montezuma, or to a still undiscernible world of
the future. In silence they walked, with an
occasional wailing; the bells stopped their beating, syncopating and stopping; the wailing grew
louder. Then all became silent, as the figures
dissolved into the darkness of the empty cave-like
churches.

We had forgotten that it was Maundy Thursday,
and that the Easter processions, better in this
neighbourhood than anywhere else in Italy, were
already beginning.

The proprietors, when we found them again,
had finished their luncheon. They had been in time
. . . delicious. . . . There had, unfortunately, been
one disturbance. The Portuguese had remarked
on the excellence of the bread, and one of them,

without intending any insinuation, had replied, "Yes, it is good; it is *white* bread!" This Il Moro had taken as a mean reflection on his colouring, and considerable trouble had ensued. Fortunately there was with them at lunch a most charming man, the chief wine-merchant in the district, the owner of cellars that were catacomb-like in their extent and intricacy. This gentleman had somehow or other smoothed over the difficulty, had asked them all to accompany him round his domains and to taste each variety of wine which he manufactured. This offer they had accepted, on our behalf as well as their own. The afternoon was thus spent in cool and slumbrous labyrinths.

Survivals

It was on our return from Gallipoli, making a second halt at Soleto, that we encountered two curious survivals. We went into a church which we had failed to see on our first visit, to discover that it possessed a most delightful and unusual painted ceiling, an enchanting affair recalling in almost equal proportions the Byzantine conventions and the art of Douanier Rousseau. It might well have been painted by a naïve artist of the fourteenth century. But the executant's signature was prettily festooned in one corner of it, and, below, the date 1864! The same generation, then, as the great Douanier. And pondering on the amusing and exquisite simplicity of that artist's work, we reflected how Italian he was in feeling. Of the later masters of nineteenth - century *French* painting—which, in fact, was world-painting—Rousseau is as essentially the painter for the religious, as Cézanne is the artist for painters and Seurat the one whose work means most to poets. Rousseau's pictures, penetrated by a rhythm that only the pure spirit of a child could have detected and fastened down, are, like those of Fra Angelico, the work of a most gifted innocent. It is the art of a child who paints as well and naturally as others dance or walk, and with a vision of his own that can never be spoilt. Fra Angelico has been made a "*beato*" by the Catholic Church, and it seems only fair that a similar compliment should be decreed to the Douanier, whose vision was equally blissful and saintly.

There are those, we believe, who pretend to think that this middle-aged Customs-House officer deliberately set out to paint in a premeditated and even archaistic fashion; but it is incredible. He had, obviously, a natural longing to paint, which would not be gainsaid, and himself was utterly unable to see the oddity of his mind or manner. He set out to paint the equivalent of an Academy picture. This was his object—for to the pure all things are pure. He admired that form of art as much as any other, because, when looking at anything, he was no doubt able to invest it with his own personality. Faced, indeed, with the gaudy pretentious canvases of the Salon and professional portrait-painters, he was unable to distinguish in them any difference from his own work. That was the sort of thing he longed to do, and subsequently he would like to be crowned officially and academically with laurel, for, as we have said, he saw the works, however atrocious, of other artists, with a divine and humble vision that purified those objects even as it was responsible for the happy beauty of his own creations. This naturally made of him as bad a critic as he was a good artist. While Cézanne knew exactly what he wanted, and for ever, sometimes even clumsily, stumbled after it, persevered and persevered, lost his temper, threw his picture into a hedge, or slit it with a knife from end to end, and then started on the same subject all over again, Rousseau, with no thought for the morrow's art, just painted away, quite happy, contented, and unaware of the nature of his own excellence. In his spare time he played the violin, gave lessons on that instrument to a pupil, an old gentleman in a top-hat, and every Sunday evening entertained a small party. To these gatherings, jealously guarded, came all the great painters of the period, and many of those of to-day—Picasso for one—who were then students. Beer was handed round, and the pupil was the only non-artist who was allowed to attend, and sometimes he and his teacher would perform on their violins for the pleasure of the guests. At this time Rousseau's pictures were selling for five francs each, but it does not appear to have depressed him in any way. He just went on painting.

Everything Rousseau touched, whether it was the intensely depressing silver wedding of a French bourgeois couple, or such an allegorical picture as *Europe renders Homage to France*, he makes holy by the simplicity of his vision, a simplicity unknown in Europe since the passing of the Primitives ; nor can the occasional absurdity of it ever detract from the holiness of his art. He was naïve and simple, but also he was a born artist. To be sure of this it is only necessary to compare his works with those of the ordinary naïve, the votive paintings, for instance, that are hung up in Italian chapels. For with this, as with any other species of artist, it is the quality of the artistry that is in the end important, and to be naïve alone is no qualification.

Europe renders Homage to France is very typical of the Douanier's art. It is painted on a fairly large, long canvas. On a platform, flanked by six flower-pots, in only five of which are plants growing, stands France, personified by the usual female in a tricolour cap, and with a lion couchant at her side. Behind her, hat in hand (for she takes but little notice of them), are the late King Edward, the Czar, the Kaiser, and the Emperor Francis Joseph, supported by a rather negligible chorus of Balkan monarchs and Teutonic princelings. On the right is a giant-stride, a-flutter with bunting, and with its aid children are whirling round in the air, at singular but happy angles. Behind them, looking out on them from a row of mean houses, are the various pale and drawn faces of the workers, clustered at the windows like white pansies. The six flower-pots that we have mentioned rise up in the foreground. Each one is labelled in large letters, the first " Liberty," the second " Fraternity," while the third one (and this is significant) is labelled " Equality "—but the plant is missing and the empty pot stands there gaping and forlorn! For Rousseau was an artist and knew better: in that particular "tenet of democracy" he had no faith. Liberty, yes; Fraternity, yes; Equality, no! . . . Nothing should ever induce him to paint-in the last flower. Yet, what is still more suggestive, if the plant had been put in, it would have spoiled the whole design. Fra Angelico, too, had he been a modern democrat, would have refused " Equality " to the multitude; and similarly the absence of it would have helped the composition of his picture. In such a combination of inevitable, unconscious art and intense feeling lies hidden the whole essence of naïve beauty.

Still talking of the Douanier and his innocence, we enter a courtyard to look at the vista beyond. And glancing round at the wall we saw another survival, another example of child-art. It was a drawing of a Punchinello : loose white clothes, high white cap slanting back, black mask and beak, and all the other correct attributes of that ancient tribe. It was equivalent to the discovery on an English wall of a drawing of King Arthur by a child—for it was distinctly the drawing of a child, and executed only a few days previously. Perhaps the love of Punchinello is so engrained in the people here, because they so much resemble him in physique and character. They are taller, more stoutly-built than most Italians, with more prominent noses and rougher features—nearer to the Roman than to the modern Italian in type.

Whether there are still travelling Punchinello theatres in Puglia it is difficult to tell; probably there are, for these companies visit such towns as Amalfi and Salerno. In Naples there still exist two or three rather dirty, small theatres where there is a regular Punchinello performance in dialect. Formerly there were many of them, patronised by the lazzaroni; and at the Museum at San Martino the authorities have recently built up a scene, with dummy figures, from one of the older theatres.

Great art has also recently seized on the same motif, for one of the best of the Russian ballets is *Polichinelle*. The scenery for this was designed by Picasso, while the music, founded on Pergolesi, has numerous additions by Stravinski, also responsible for the orchestration, the scene

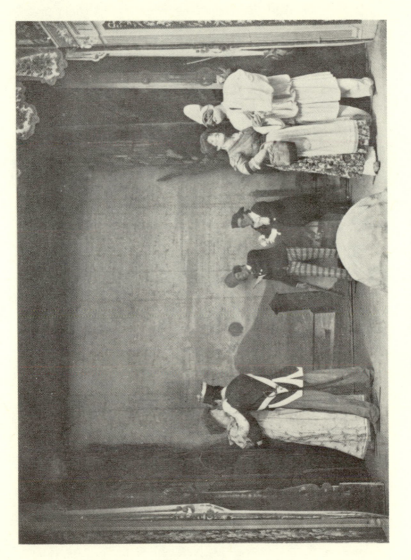

SCENE FROM A PUNCHINELLO THEATRE
Museo di San Martinos, Naples

being placed in a Neapolitan town of the late seventeenth or early eighteenth century. If it be true, in addition, that Charlie Chaplin intends to throw away his baggy trousers, his cane and billycock hat, and discard even his moustache, in order to adopt the still more conventional garb and gesture of a Punchinello, we may yet see a revived Italian comedy conquer the cinema—for Chaplin, even in his present-day clothes, belongs essentially to that order of humour. Meanwhile, it is comforting to know that in the far, small towns, Punchinello, whether as a member of a travelling company or in the guise of a marionette, holds his own with Charlie.

The art of the puppet-theatre, formerly carried to the highest pitch of achievement in the old Kingdom of the Two Sicilies, is now in a state of decadence. There is, of course, the Art Marionette Theatre of Rome ; but however admirable and enchanting its performances, this is a highly-conscious affair, with a special public—a last blossom put out while the tree itself withers at the root. For the puppet-theatre has lost its grip on the people, and by its very nature it ought to be a popular, and not a specialised, art-form. Even before the war very few of the old theatres existed ; to-day there is but a handful left, to be found in the most wretched quarters of Naples, Palermo, and Catania. Strange temples of an ancient art they are, these small, hot, dusty theatres, with galleries painted in the style more often associated with votive pictures. There is usually a decorated stall, bright blue and red, white and grey, clangorous with brass ladles and plates, and loaded with loathsome little glasses of lemonade. Pampas-grass plumes at each corner add to it the air of a gaily-painted hearse. In the autumn the solitary lemonade is augmented by heaped-up plates of prickly-pears. This fruit, cheap enough for the children to buy, is very lovely to look at—like a blood-orange in tone—for it is sold ready-peeled, and the angular flat surfaces cut with a knife make of it a faceted gem more than a fruit.

For months the marionettes perform the historic dramas of Tasso and Ariosto : in these dark and fusty holes the classics make a final stand against the oncoming waves of Northern and Western inanity, against *The Dollar Princess*, the Beauty Chorus, the Joy-Plank and the democratic noisy dadaism of Mr Alfred Noyes and—if such there be —his like. On this reduced scale, upon this little stage, the Crusader once more prances to the wars on a very armorial horse and defeats the infidel Saracen, while the man who pulls the wires declaims chivalresque sentiments in a noble voice, much as did International Finance in our own dear Late Great. It is a fine performance, still full of medieval romance. The Paladins clank about the stage in shining armour, and from their helmets bravely flow magenta plumes. Again the beloved one is rescued, this time (O horrible fate !)

In the Heel of Italy

on the verge, the very doorstep so to speak, of a harem. Once again, though not by any means finally, the knight, fully equipped, hacks off the heathen head of the Saracen. The latter is presented to us, as was the Turk of the nursery, with an enormous turban and ferocious curving blade. The movements are abrupt; some legs appear to be rather on the swivel, but it is impossible to get away from the illusion of reality, impossible to believe that these figures are only dolls eighteen inches in height. Evening after evening the same serial drama unrolls, perhaps continuing for as long as three months. Then follows another epic of the same species; the classics are taken turn by turn. The audience, which, up to the middle of last century, consisted of all the richest and most intelligent bandits and beggars of the Two Sicilies—men apparently of real critical judgment, and who, though unable to read, were possessed of a genuine love for the classics, which they learnt in this way by heart, would exchange intelligent remarks during the performance on the accent and declamation of the man behind the scenes — has now sunk to a few very unclean children and one or two adult simpletons or village-idiots. Yet Madame Giglioli tells us in her most interesting volume (*Naples in 1799*— published by Murrays) that the revolutionary Government of the first Parthenopean Republic sought to influence popular opinion through the

medium of the marionette theatre. It is the same
idea of "propaganda" which now induces the
Bolsheviks to make an equivalent use of the
theatre and cinema in Russia. And the action
of the Neapolitan revolutionaries was as much a
tribute to the power of the puppet-show, as that
of the Bolsheviks is a testimonial to the ineradic-
able nature of the theatre-habit in Russia. It
was felt by them that if they could democratise
the puppets, and introduce a propagandist element,
they could influence the politically-backward com-
munities in big cities as well as in small towns
and villages, where otherwise no idea would penetrate. Thus, only, could they reach a public which
could not read or write ; for the Bourbons had
never encouraged such new-fangled practices.

In place, then, of the traditional heroic dramas,
the rebels attempted to substitute others, in which
great attention would be paid to the tyranny of
kings and queens, especially of runaway ones ;
white-powdered wigs would be made fun of, and
the Spirit of Freedom would be shown moving
gradually southward from France and releasing
the waiting peoples. Bonaparte, already engaged
on his monotonous career of conquest, would be
presented as the Champion of Liberty, while the
detested Nelson, who was at that moment at
Palermo, in the disreputable company of the King
and Queen of Naples and Lady Hamilton, would
be finally exposed as the tool of vile and corrupt

tyranny. All these details were well planned, but of no avail, since the love of the classics was so strong in the illiterate that they refused to witness any other dramas than those to which they were used. Now, alas! the puppet-theatres are empty, and with them passes one of the last links between Ancient Rome and Modern Europe.

Meanwhile, we need not despair; the study of Charlie Chaplin is quite as important as that of any ancient poet for the modern child, and of infinitely more value for his master. Let the educationalists suppress forcibly the pernicious habit of compulsory games for pupils in English schools, and instead institute compulsory visits to the cinema for the masters. Each teacher should be forced to see Charlie Chaplin at least twice a week. He might then learn to appreciate the advantage that genius has over mediocrity, the importance of Art over all other things, and the intense sympathy of genius for the weak and oppressed. But perhaps even now the school-master steals away secretly to watch Charlie on the films; for Art often lures on those whom it means ultimately to destroy. Thus Rousseau and Voltaire fascinated the polite world of the eighteenth century, and Shakespeare still has an irresistible appeal for the budding actor-manager.

ii

The Miracle

EVEN before a water-spout had transformed the lovely garden of the hotel into an avalanche of mud, sweeping it down into the sea, that was now dark and glossy as a raven, Amalfi was in the winter rather free from visitors. The hotel had formerly been a monastery, and about it and the pendent terrace, a quarter of a mile in length and fronting one of the most beautiful views in Southern Europe, there still clung something of monastic calm and seclusion.

In the spring, however, there would be a Gothic Invasion from the north, old English ladies abloom with bugle and jet—each clasping her Prayer Book, a volume by Ruskin, and a small packet of cough drops, with arthritic and knotted knuckles—would sit for hours in the vaulted sitting-room below. This room was embellished with a framed poem by Longfellow, a gilt-framed portrait of Mr Gladstone, and a mantelshelf draped with a hanging fringe in the form of a net, with round red woollen blobs, marking each intersection and swinging at the outer edge of the whole contrivance. These three properties, indeed, would make even an elderly Tory feel at home. Alas, one day, in a frenzy, we flew at the mantelshelf and, almost before we had realised our crime, had torn off red bobble after red bobble and cast it into the deep blue sea below. It is difficult to explain the nature of the transport that, seizing us all of a sudden, forced us to perpetrate this outrage. It was partly a Pyrrhic and Dionysian fury, partly the fanatic spirit of a Savonarola. Luckily the sea was at too great a distance under for us to be haunted by these red-wool apparitions, popping up to the surface like so many reproachful eyes of drowning men.[1] Nevertheless a panic ensued. The marble mantelpiece was fortunately built with its back to the light; but even then the gaps, with the naked white marble peeping through, were very visible. An attempt to mend it would be useless, for the bobbles were gone. An explanation to the management (and more especially to one so kind) would be too painful. With extraordinary resource we set-to, and since we could not replace the network or the hanging globes, instead, we traced the shadows of the missing blobs and the network connecting them in pencil upon the marble mantelpiece. Under electric light it was impossible to notice the deception, though sometimes, on a very fine day, we would see one of the old ladies

[1] Or so we can picture the open eyes of the murdered Admiral Caracciolo, as borne along by each successive wave, his hair flying behind him, he approached ever nearer to the frigate of King Ferdinand, who was morally responsible for his death.

looking at it suspiciously, severely. Yet the management never discovered their loss; and when we returned to the hotel eighteen months later the mantelpiece was still in the same condition.

Apart, then, from this more permanent squadron of old ladies that we have mentioned, there was in the spring a continual and shifting population. In March, a month which is here acknowledged to be the rainy season, a horde of tourists would descend every evening, like a swarm of very noisy transatlantic locusts, devouring all the oranges and tearing up the flowers in the garden. Laden with their withered booty, they would leave early the next morning, to be succeeded by an equivalent swarm in the evening. Always they would discuss the same questions. They would deplore the dirt of the Neapolitan populace, and the lack of sanitation in Southern Italy—for it is now supposed that constant-hot-water and a telephone constitute culture; and they were incapable of understanding that washing, however desirable as an ideal, only became a convention in Europe after the French Revolution. All the old things it is customary for American visitors to admire, Gothic cathedrals and Rood Screens, were constructed by an utterly unwashed (and therefore, according to modern standards, backward) population. And those who now spend their money on plumbing, formerly bought pictures or built palaces. Only infidels like the Turks and Saracens

The Miracle

washed in the Middle Ages. The exception to this rule were the Byzantine Greeks, who had inherited such decadent habits from the late Roman Empire. But in Italy the coming of Christianity, with its hair-shirts and hermits, had quickly blotted out the memory of any former cleanliness. Indeed the whole spirit of early and medieval Western Christianity was to encourage the spirit, and to chasten and neglect the body.

In the Palazzo Ruffulo, however, at Ravello just above us, there was one of the only medieval bathrooms in Europe. With a dome shaped like a cantaloup melon, it dates back to the thirteenth or twelfth century, and both the architecture of it and the habit it indulged, point to the Saracen influence in this neighbourhood.

American bathrooms, we suppose, are more numerous than our own; with a conscious air of superiority the crowd for hours discussed plumbing, as once Englishmen used to discuss politics, till every old lady, in her enthusiasm, seemed crowned with a tiara of white-painted pipes. The next morning the horde would set off for Pæstum (not much of the bathroom spirit about that, incidentally!), and in the evening another swarm would settle in the hotel and the same conversation would ensue.

Throughout this month of March there would be a perpetual sirocco, though, when it did not actually rain, the world would look peculiarly

Discursions

lovely, large and strange; for the humidity of the air gave a distinct and precise outline to everything. Behind us, against the dark slate sky, the limestone cliffs rose towering over the terraces. The deep yellow light, which here accompanies this kind of weather, would display the very varied green tones given out by orange- and lemon-trees, myrtle, ilex and cactus, and a thousand fleshy-foliaged wild plants on the verge of breaking into blossom. Under this theatrical, rather menacing illumination it would be perceived that this verdancy artfully concealed a whole scale of colour; that there was as much difference between the clamorous insistent-yellow-green of some of the wild plants and the deep mysterious grape-bloom tone of the ilex, between the polished bronze of the orange leaf, the translucent green-amber of the cactus, and the ashen green of some of the rock plant leaves, that were almost like donkeys' ears in their furred greyness, as there is usually between red and blue, yellow and magenta. The air was unnaturally saturated with the scent of orange blossom, and the sea, which generally manifested a very gay palette, was now sombre, sinister as a magpie's wing, blue and black, broken by a sudden and unaccountable curveting of white horses. This flat expanse of ominous colour formed the appropriate foreground for the water-spouts that would be seen occasionally spinning their golden tops on the horizon, over and across which they would

The Miracle

travel with the fabled speed of a witch on her broomstick. Away on the left an immense spur of dusky hills could be seen running on for ever into the sea and, though these were so dark in colour, every detail of the coast was clear and definite. The temples at Pæstum, almost opposite us, and here the test of visibility, could be realised more distinctly than on the finest day. The whole scene, and especially the fantastic mountains behind us, which rose straight up from the sea, and proudly displayed every natural device of which limestone alone is capable—caves, grottos, stalactites, arches, bastions, flying buttresses, towers, pinnacles, doorways and windows, all trellised with wreaths of the most verdant luxuriance—seemed set, under this light, for the chief personage in some dark and supernatural drama—demon, sea-serpent, or dragon; but none ever came; only the visitors, more and more of them, descended each evening upon the hotel.

In the winter, though, it was quite otherwise. The town would sink back into its usual rather rough and lonely life. In the day the sky would be very blue, the earth at night very cold. The whitewashed cloister, of which but half was left, one shorter side looking down on to the fallen cliff and the sea below it, would glitter frostily in the hot sun. The lovely arches, pointed and interlacing, at once both Gothic and Saracen—the place where the East and North winds met—sprang up to-day so lightly into the air on their little white marble columns, that it seemed as if their cold radiance must be fashioned from snow or ice, and the explanation of the missing part of the cloister, thus, not that the earth beneath and the cave above had given way, but that it had softly melted and run down beneath the rays of the ardent sun. Looking up through the arches, one could see an incredible and unbelievable perspective of unclouded sky and overhanging rock, which, rising straight up above the cloister, was covered, as far as the eye could travel, with clinging weeds and jonquils in full flower.

The long white corridors, which yet retained an air of monastic severity and asceticism, would be empty and soundless, except for the warm chatter of the servants penetrating from the kitchen and floor below. The terrace, too, was deserted save for the presence of a Neapolitan lady of about thirty-five years of age and rather weak in the head, who still insisted on wearing her hair down her back in two long black pigtails — a habit which particularly displeased the hall-porter, who had discovered from careful observation that if she indulged it three days running a spell of rainy weather was the sequel. Thus there were frequent and secret signs made against the evil eye. It was, in fact, a singularly irritating appearance, and the tails, hanging at the back, made her head immense and uncouth, like that of some Easter

The Miracle

Island figure ; and this capillary extravagance was especially annoying at the moment when every other woman of her age in the whole of Europe was intent on one thing, and one thing only—the cutting off and flinging away of her hair! Her family had placed her in the hotel, and kept on postponing the date of her return to them, maddened obviously both by this trick, and by the child-like inflection of her voice, which would have enraged even a saint.

At this season there were not many flowers on the terrace, but the long tufts, like mauve lamb-tails, of some unknown blossom, lolled over the edge, showing up vibratingly against the sea, which was lively in its play of colour as a living thing, full of moving radiance as a butterfly. The mauve of this flower, indeed, exactly matched certain streaks in the sea, while it set off other tones of blue and purple. Far away, towards Salerno, there were little clusters of boats with white sails outspread to match the butterflies on the flowers, and from this distance no bigger. Behind them rose Monte Alburno, powdered with snow, so that the shadows in its clefts embraced all these grape-blue tones of the sea, while its curious outline, razor-sharp yet broken, was glittering as though it were a thing of crystal that had been cut in facets to display the depths of its translucency. The coast between it and the sea was a haze, and the temples were hidden beneath the golden pall.

Discursions

On the higher terraces, that mounted up to the wild garden behind, the oranges were not yet ripe, though their globes were already yellow. A borrowed radiance seemed to emanate from them, as though, like the earth, they were smaller planets deriving light from the sun, and in their turn casting it among the mysterious interplanetary leaves that surrounded them.

A thousand steps below, on the road, people could be seen moving like ants. From here it was possible to examine their movements impersonally, to watch their convolutions as one observes the manœuvres of a flattened heap of ants under a glass slab. On the whole, they appeared pleased with themselves. They would stop to speak, and then move swiftly about again, carrying on their heads the most enormous loads, great bundles of wooden planks and young saplings; a bed, or even a piano. Old women, with grey hair and bunched-up peasant skirts, with bare feet, and a tall staff in one hand to guide them, would mount the steps up to the hotel with an exceptional grace and dignity of movement, balancing a whole felled forest on their heads. The amiable village-idiot, who was for ever singing or smiling, was walking slowly on the road below declaiming, laughing, and supporting on his head an earthenware pitcher. He would talk to everyone he passed; then a child would come darting up the steps with a basketful of small sword-fish, with their steel-blue pointed beaks, and bodies which were in colour an electric mingling of blue and silver. Then other provisions would be brought up, large wicker baskets full of grapes that had been soaked and boiled in wine and wrapped in vine and lemon leaves, giving out a sharp aromatic scent. These were from Calabria. But the most curious sight of all was to watch the Archbishop, and the antics of those who met him on the road. Escorted by one or two lesser dignitaries, he would stroll with great importance, and rather slowly, along the road below, and all the people passing him went through the ceremony of bowing and kissing the ring. These ritual capers were peculiarly insect-like.

Life in the winter was a constant routine. In the afternoon the zampognari would come up to play before the Presepio [1] in the chapel and afterward they would give a short concert outside in the cloister. Toward the end of November these shepherds first appear from their homes in the mountains. They play in private chapels every day up to Christmas, when they return home, having earned enough money to live in idleness for the rest of the year. Indeed, not only do

---

[1] Presepio : a model of the Nativity displaying the Madonna and Child, the three kings of the East, the shepherds, angels and other persons incident to the sacred story, but treating it as one native to South Italy. The zampognari would be shown playing, the peasants would be wearing their local dresses, and in the older models the kings of the East would be wearing periwigs !

Discursions

they play in every chapel, but in nearly every house in these villages; for every respectable family owns a presepio. The one in the hotel was a particularly fine example of the seventeenth century, and all the little figures were in their original dresses. The men playing in front of this model were precisely like the zampognari represented in it. They wore long grey cloaks; one carried a huge goatskin bagpipe, the other a short wooden horn. Usually these two chief performers are accompanied by a third man, who sings the hymn of the Nativity in the traditional way—for every peasant woman teaches her son to sing as her father did when she was a child.

When the zampognari left the chapel and played in the cloister, the latter would become alive with sound as though a swarm of bees had descended upon it. The buzzing and droning notes would creep into every cell and crevice of the building, and of the rock above. The latter, full as it is of hidden caves and grottos, resounded with all these winging notes, which fluttered round them, redoubling their drone, and discovering every crevice and hollow place in which they could nestle to beat and drum their wings. This music is very obviously the natural and native music of the country. The limestone crags might have been constructed especially for the purpose of echoing and filtering such strange harmonies. Among these mountains they carry for an incredible

GALATINA : CHURCH DOOR

The Miracle

distance, and every village sprawling over the edge of a rocky shelf is now clamorous with these harsh Doric sounds, while even the old shepherd in goat-skin trousers, leading his flock down the headlong hill through boulders and young trees, sings the same hymn as he goes.

Meanwhile the cloister, from which so much noise swells up, is full of people. The servants, who all belong to the district, have clustered together in one corner. The fat chef has come out and offers to sing. Fortunata, the housemaid, who has been in the service of the landlord's family for over sixty years, who can neither read nor write, and is reputed to sleep with her entire fortune in a tin box under her bed, smiles with a toothless grace and claps her hands like a child. The two hall-porters, one of the hotel itself, the other from the lodge attached to it at the bottom of the steps, are both here together. Usually they assume to each other a distant manner; for they share a mutual secret. They are, in fact, father and son, but are victims of a morbid fear that if visitors are allowed to find this out they will economise and make the same tip (or, rather, " commensurate donation," in the dignified language of Mr Baedeker) serve for both of them. However, in their pleasure at the music they forget their pretence, and address each other openly as father and son. Soon the music stops and the pipers leave; but as they descend the steep flight of steps they again begin playing, the musician sheltering the bag under his cloak; and their strange wailings can be heard very clearly as they climb down through tunnel and rocky passage into the town below. Upon the terrace it is evident that we have now reached the ceremonial stage of our journey through space, and our little globe's pompous farewell to the sun is just beginning. The detail of this parting is precisely the same on every fine evening, and continues for some thirty minutes, during which the farewell becomes ever more painful and strained, until it is like seeing a friend off at a railway station. The sea flushes a deep wine colour; the white Luna Convent on the point opposite has changed from white to gold and crimson, and Monte Alburno's planes of snow are offered as so many mirrors in which the parting guest can see reflected his mutable glory. The other hills are russet and blue, with golden crowns, and the whole earth is enjoying its most ostentatious moment, when the attention of the human element is instantly attracted away from all this splendour by a sudden stir of excitement below. All the little cabs in the town rattle at once toward the quay, for the event of the day is at hand. The small steamer from Naples, narrow as a shark, has been sighted and will soon arrive. Every window in the hotel is at once flung open, and everybody in it stands with elbows on the window ledge, shouting, regardless of the sun that is still waving his farewells, dangling coloured streamers of cloud into the very windows, daring the earth to charge it with his blood-red mantle in the manner of matador and bull. We take no notice of this sudden change of tactics, but remain gaping out of our many windows. The boat is drawn up by this time and every detail of its short cruise is already known up in the hotel, inquiries having been shouted from the hotel to the roadway, from the roadway to the quay, from the quay to the boat, and the answer returned by the same method in reversed order. There has been a bad motor smash in Naples; the Duke of Aosta is slightly better to-day; there are two English ladies and a young American gentleman with tortoiseshell-rimmed glasses coming up to the hotel. The others, two Danes and an Austrian, are supposed to be going to the Pension below. One man left the boat at Capri, and may be expected to-morrow —under God's protection.

The three visitors climb slowly up the steps, stopping every now and then, turning round to watch the highly-coloured antics of the sun. When they are within five steps of the top, the servants, who have been laughing and shouting inquiries, adopt a less provincial and more formal air, but the windows are not finally shut, nor does the conversation — though temporarily interrupted— actually finish, until the sun has fluttered his last farewell, and "Barba Nera" is seen strutting up the steps, with the black leather postbag hanging from a strap across his broad shoulders.

"Barba Nera" was an interesting character, the local equivalent of Old Moore: for a suitable gratuity he would prophesy fine weather for any excursion, and he did it with a manner. He was very short, and it was therefore more than ever necessary for him to assume dignity at the proper Delphic moment, to wear his prophet's mantle with a suitable swagger. He would throw up his head, holding out one arm in a warning way, while a look of great cunning and vinous prescience would come into his round button eyes. His sentences he would enunciate with all the fervour of a prophet, and with that clear-cut technique and feeling for the colour of words which is the mark of the great actor or orator. His whole appearance at these moments became somewhat oracular, for his face was like that of an intelligent, very elderly ventriloquist's dummy with a Victor Emmanuel moustache slung across the upper lip; his round eyes were slightly protruding and black, like those of a shrimp, and one felt that through the open mouth some hidden and wiser voice was giving utterance. Alas, it was usually the rollicking voice of the good god Bacchus! But if "Barba Nera" was never sober, yet at least he was never—or very seldom—quite drunk.

He had begun life, it was said, as a brigand, but had retired many years ago and taken to light

The Miracle

and odd jobs. His home was a small house half way down the hill toward the town, and it was his duty to carry up the post to the hotel twice a day. Though his stature was very small, he was broad-shouldered and of an immense strength—so that, in spite of the fact that he was over seventy years of age, he would think nothing of lifting up an enormous American trunk twice as large as himself, swinging it on to his back, or if possible on to his head, and then proceeding with it up the thousand steps to the hotel. These feats, however—so one was given to understand — made him unusually thirsty.

"Barba Nera" was extremely well known in the district and very popular. And he adopted an air of proprietorship. He was the impresario of the surrounding coast, and his effects were beautifully staged and produced. His voice was deep and loud, and if one met him on the steps and inquired the name or profession of someone passing below on the road, or even farther down on the quay, he would quickly, and with an acute sense of characterisation, explain that person's history and peculiarities. Then holding up the cup of his hands to his mouth, he would form a loud speaker of it, and his voice would traverse any distance easily, and be audible. He would question the individual and proceed to put him through his paces, forcing him to display any latent eccentricity, to revolve through that accustomed hoop which himself had so lately and graphically described.

The wife of this little brigand, a handsome, grey-haired peasant woman, shared her husband's social and convivial inclinations. Between them, it was maintained, they thought nothing of "putting away" four litres of red wine a day. Spirits, however, they regarded as immoral and never touched. The amount they drank was a source of great pride to the locality, and people would say, " Nowadays the young drink spirits ; they won't live to be the age of Maria and Barba Nera. Good red wine never did anybody any harm." Extremely kind parents, they were excessively devoted to their children : their youngest daughter was at the time of our last visit suffering from typhoid fever, which made her an interesting figure in the town life ; and the one idea of her parents was that I should meet her before that fever had worn off. Wouldn't I come in at once ? She would, the little one, though delirious, be delighted to see me. . . .

Besides the pocket-money they earned by odd jobs, this curious couple derived a regular income from America. Though their family was a large one, they had in addition, out of pious gratitude for the recovery of their eldest son from a dangerous illness, adopted a foundling. Him they had treated in every way as their own child and had given as good an education as it was within their power

The Miracle

to procure. When he grew up he emigrated to America, where he now earned more than all their other children put together. He never forgot their kindness, and every month dispatched a sum of money to his benefactors : thus the dollars earned in that parched half-continent were spent in the less arid atmosphere of Italian *trattorias*.

" Barba Nera " was by now at the top of the steps, and was prophesying fine weather, with a little snow on the hills, for another fortnight. It was a well-known fact, he added, that St Andrew, the patron saint of Amalfi, always brought fine weather to his town—and soon it would be his feast day. Meanwhile dusk had fallen, and since it was a warm, calm night, fishing-boats had put out to sea, each one carrying a blazing star to attract their prey, until the whole sea was clustered with these gently-swinging constellations. It seemed as if a flight of gigantic fireflies had taken to this other element, as though the fluttering flames were caught and struggling in the salt and scaly nets intended for the fish. When the early morning light came, these sea-stars faded out, and it was necessary for men to devise new tricks for the bewilderment of foolish marine creatures ; thus as the dead stars floated back to the shore, more boats put out—but this time it was a sound and not a light that was to lure the fish into the waiting nets. When far enough out, the fisherman would rest his oars, and sitting in the stern of the little boat so that his back continued the line of it, he would thump the side of it with his hand or with a wooden club, hammering out a regular but enraging rhythm. One could imagine that if, taking a violin, the fisherman had played to the silver-flashing denizens of the ocean one of Kreisler's waltzes, or Weber's romantic *Invitation à la Valse*, the fish would have come leaping and bounding into his boat. But why this maddening clatter should attract anything — let alone a fish — it was difficult to explain! Yet, in the early hours of the morning, the sea was covered with these small boats, and resonant with their monotonous wooden drummings. From this distance up in the air, man and boat appeared to belong to each other, to be part of the same mechanism of nature, to be so many water-beetles creeping over the even surface of the water.

"Barba Nera" had been correct in his weather forecast. Though the mainland behind the mountains and behind the coast was no doubt frost-black and hung with icicles like a Christmas tree, here above the sea on these rocky shelves of limestone it was as warm as if one was on a shelf in a green-house. Yet the climate did not appear to be artificial, as does that of the French Riviera. It matched, exquisitely, the sea and landscape, which were more defined and more varied in shape and colour than that of the Riviera. And after an English landscape, what a relief to be in one that could be stylised so simply and easily. Any good artist could find a convention for it, whereas the English landscape is almost impossible to stylise, and can only be rendered æsthetically in the terribly realistic manner of Constable, that great painter and most detestable artist.

For several days before the *festa*, the people of Amalfi were growing ever more excited, and on the great day itself the whole district was seething with pleasurable emotion. At an early hour the roads were packed with peasants from the neighbouring villages, and all the country people were decked out in their most fashionable clothes, the men having discarded for the day their more sombre and effective cloaks and scarves. The outer piazza of the town, planted with an avenue of wizened palm-trees, ranged so near the waves that the continual spray and salt breath had cured them, as though they were kippers, and transformed them into lifeless everlasting plants, was full of trestles and the sound of trumpets. Everyone in all the town was trying to sell something. Young men stood up on a platform, their frizzed-out hair standing up from their foreheads, shouting, making fabulous orations and the most superb gestures in their anxiety to induce the crowd to buy their new winter-stuffs. Even at this early hour the sun flashed down unexpectedly strong wings upon the piazza, so that shouting and waving must have been a warm and heavy business. There were many sweet-stalls for the children, and huge baskets of fruits, fresh and dried. Fortunes were being told by a young Sicilian, and barrel-organs were playing without stopping. A cockatoo sat on top of the instrument, and as it played nodded its head in rhythm, while little operatic figures, the size of a man's finger, gesticulated inside a glass case. From the narrow streets, which were pouring people down into the inner piazza, the bagpipes could be heard droning continually. Going through the low, whitewashed thirteenth-century arch from the outer to the inner square, the sound and rhythm dashed up at us with redoubled volume. The cathedral steps jut out boldly in a long flight to the square below, and these alone were empty, for every other inch of space was occupied by the crowd, and by the merchants of sweets and gingerbread. The sky above was framed in by the tall limestone mountains, and the houses, washed white, blue, rose-pink or terra-cotta, climbed up the steep cliffs for ever. Some were set down on little terraces; others were actually fitted into the mouths of caverns, while stalactites hung down, touching the roof as though the teeth of some gigantic creature were closing on them, and the little houses would soon disappear like Jonah, engulfed by a dark and monstrous belly. The houses, pretty, graceful and artificial, contrasted with these primeval caverns that might well have been the stables for a former race of centaurs—stables from which a troop of them could come galloping and cantering down to bathe in the sea, splashing, puffing and snorting through the fretted foam. Or again, such a grotto would seem eminently fitted for the housing of a Chinese dragon; out of it, doubtless, the beast would issue forth, bellowing horribly, breathing rockets of fire, rolling from side to side with a nautical gait, and then, clear of the cave, would open out vast bat-like wings and sail away, away, over the sea, stopping for a moment to alight, as does a bird, on the top of Monte Alburno, which seemed, indeed, still to retain on its surface the indentation of some such ferocious claws.

In the centre of the crowd rose a fountain, bearing on it the marble image of St Andrew tied to his cross. From his right arm dangled a small shoal of aluminium or tin fishes, very glittering in the light, but not so shimmeringly silver as the real ones that lay near-by, piled up in huge baskets. These effigies are hung up by the fishermen before they go out, as a bribe to St Andrew to give them his aid, and bless them with a big catch. It is said that where the old piazza—the one that disappeared under the terrible inundation which destroyed Amalfi as a sea-power in the fourteenth century—stands, covered with limpets, while forests of seaweed float in at the gaping windows and the gardens are full of red and blue sea anemones, it is possible on a fine day to distinguish a similar though more beautiful statue of

Discursions

St Andrew. We asked why it was not dredged up, but the fishermen replied that it would be impolite to disturb his holiness, their patron saint, whose right arm was still stretched out below the ocean to bless them and to secure for them as heavy a scaly harvest as their nets would bear.

Though it was still early, "Barba Nera," the centre of a crowd, was already flushed and prophesying in the piazza. The people were gradually edging back, however, for soon the procession would start. The Byzantine doors of the cathedral, green-bronze with silver inlay, were suddenly swung open, and out marched the procession with the Archbishop at its head, bowing and blessing. He performed the ceremony to perfection, with hieratic and sphinx-like dignity. Crowned with his mitre, with his high crook held in one hand and his long train supported behind him, slowly, yet with no sign of shame or awkwardness, he began to descend the steps. Not for a moment can he have feared, as would an ordinary mortal under such circumstances, a headlong tumble into the crowd below. Behind him followed many banners and sacred relics, borne by men in white robes, their heads half hidden by white cowls. Among the latter I noticed the village-idiot from Scala, who had obviously come down all this distance for the occasion, and was enjoying immensely his new rôle.

By dinner-time the procession was over; and all

The Miracle

the afternoon the children of the town fired off squibs in honour of their patron saint. Then in the evening came the chief service. Climbing up the steps to the cathedral, we noticed two men, one of whom looked rather despondent, standing at the bottom of them, looking up at the lighted windows. The cathedral was exceedingly crowded, the atmosphere that of a theatrical first night. There was an air of suppressed excitement and expectation. All the peasants from the outlying districts had come in for the event, and among them was a contingent of very strange - looking people from Nola. This town has the most fanatic population in Southern Europe, and it is there that the worship of Apollo, and the rites connected with it, still continue under a very thin disguise. There were a great number of old men sitting together, groaning with age and religious fervour, while the younger members of the congregation strolled about, talking and laughing. The cathedral was blazing with candles, and incense hung over them heavily, somewhat discolouring their flames. The centre of one arrangement of flowers and candles was the fine silver statue of St Andrew presented to the town by Philip III. of Spain : in this setting it looked very well. No doubt the silver in which it was modelled had been wrung, with tortures no less terrible than those inflicted on the saint it represents, from the wretched natives of Mexico and Peru.

Discursions

Crowds still flocked in at the wide-open doors, till the church became so full that it was difficult to move. Suddenly there was a great commotion, and a little knot of people could be seen moving through the crowd. At first it was impossible to distinguish the cause of this confusion, and we imagined that a man had been seized with illness and was being carried out. But the tumult approached us, and then we saw what it was. An old grey-haired man was crawling on hands and knees along the floor of the cathedral, like a tortoise, his head close down to it, and his tongue protruding, to touch the marble pavers which were not overclean. He was being guided—for his head was too near the floor for him to be able to see where he was going—by another old man who had fastened a long scarf to his collar and was leading him slowly toward the silver St Andrew. Right up the side of the cathedral went this queer devout procession, surrounded by the curious throng. The two old men who were the centre of it, were the ones we had noticed standing at the bottom of the steps looking up at the lighted church. The one who was now crawling in the manner we have described had attended this same service the year before, had prayed earnestly to St Andrew, and had vowed that if his prayer was granted, he would show his gratitude to the saint by climbing on all-fours up the steps and then proceeding through the cathedral on all-fours as far as the silver image,

The Miracle

literally biting the dust as he went![1] It was a horrible and interesting spectacle; for in medieval Europe, and in the England of the Middle Ages as well, such a vow was of quite common occurrence: but however disillusioned we may be about the civilisation of modern Europe, it was not the sort of performance we should expect to see in this epoch.

Soon there was a general stampede into the crypt, where the annual wonder of the " Miraculous Manna " was about to take place. The crowd down there was mostly masculine, and was so wedged together that the slightest movement was impossible. " Barba Nera " was prominent among the notables, and shepherded us for the occasion. After an interminable time the Archbishop entered. Walking slowly up to the altar, he held up what was apparently a silver-mounted glass test-tube, full of some opaque white substance, for all to see. The contents of it had to liquefy and become transparent. If the miracle did not eventuate, it was a bad omen for the town, and a year of disaster would follow. Prayers were read, and then, once more, the Archbishop held up this glass cylinder. Now the crowd began to shout. It was an application of Dr Coué's doctrines to religion. "*Credo*," they yelled, "*credo*, I believe in St Andrew and his blessed miracle. I believe.

[1] Thus the Emperor Charlemagne once crawled up the steps of St Peter's.

Discursions

I believe in St Andrew and his blessed miracle.
I believe in the Liquefaction of the Manna. I
believe. I believe." Thus they roared for ten
minutes or so; the Archbishop held up the tube
again. Nothing had happened. More prayers were
said, and then the shouting and declarations of faith
began as before. The Archbishop held up the
object of attention for the third time—and now a
great shout went up, for the manna had liquefied
and the miracle had taken place! It was a good
augury, and the crowd flowed out happily into
the fresh night air. Little did the religious people
of Amalfi suspect then that within three months
a considerable part of their town and of the
surrounding coast would be in ruins. . . .

We climbed slowly up to the white hotel—so
obviously a monastery, like those on Mount Athos
and even in distant Thibet—balanced on its rocky
shelf. By the time we had reached the top of
the steps the fireworks were beginning below.
Throwing open the window, we watched the rockets
that sprayed out on a level with us. The golden
stalks, like the fabulous plant of Jack the Giant-
Killer, leapt gaily up into the air and the fiery
blossoms were like bouquets at the windows—
bunches of red, green and yellow flowers that
faded even as they reached us.

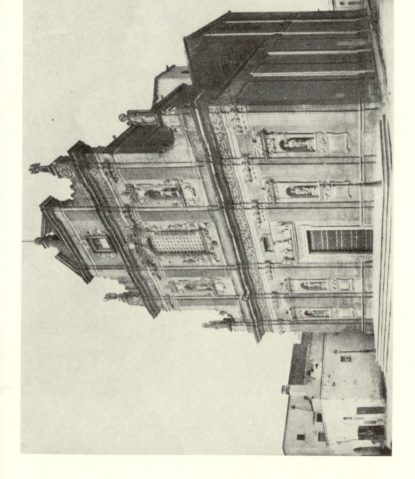

Photograph: Alinari

GALATONE: CHURCH OF THE CRUCIFIXION

iii

La Certosa di Padula

ONLY in the old realm of Naples do a few monasteries survive in a state similar to that which has existed since their foundation. And these are still allowed only because of the great tradition of learning which they embody. Yet they are only three in number.

First comes Monte Cassino, the most famous of them, founded by St Benedict in the year 529. The position is magnificent, the building impressive, and the library especially interesting; but the modern interior decoration is like that of a Wagnerian theatre. Monte Cassino has other claims to distinction besides its learning, for the town beneath supplies itinerant musicians of the barrel-organ to every town in Europe.

Next comes Monte Vergine, another enormous edifice on the top of a high hill. Here, in the summer, it is still possible to see thirty or forty thousand people climbing up the steep cliffs on their hands and knees. Unfortunately we visited it at the wrong season of the year. Below, far below at the base of the mountain, is the "Ospedaletto," an octagonal stucco building

Discursions

said to have been designed by Vanvitelli, but in reality designed by a Neapolitan architect named Vaccaro. This building was established in the eighteenth century as a rest-house for the Abbot and older monks, for the long winters on the top of a snow-bound mountain were too much, even for these men of primitive life.

The " Ospedaletto " is a most interesting example of planning, and the garden court, with its palm-trees and box hedges, against the rose-pink surface of the walls, is delightful. The interior comprises an eighteenth-century chemist's shop with a complete set of old jars, and the Royal Apartments. The latter are fine rooms, hung with magnificent Flemish tapestries of the fifteenth century, while the chairs and chandeliers, which belong to the date of the convent itself, are interesting in their way. The rooms have that curious air of echoing empty dustiness which is to be found in deserted royal palaces. This Ichabod atmosphere is increased by the pomposity of the marble placards extolling the virtues of Kings Ferdinand I. and II.

The country here is peculiarly medieval and untouched, the life of the peasant is the same as it has always been. Outside the huge door of the " Ospedaletto " was gathered a group of cringing, whining, ragged beggars, ringing the bell. After a time it was answered and a plate of macaroni was thrust through a little grating. So well acquainted was one with this scene in romantic novels and descriptions of medieval life, that it seemed almost familiar.

Third of the monasteries, and most lovely in situation, though less impressive in size than its brothers, comes La Cava. To this day one can see how such a religious house evolved, for the building is fitted into caves and grottos in the natural rock, and one can imagine the anchorite in hair-shirt, with gaunt body and long beard, first encrevicing himself here as an insect seeks refuge under a stone. The Norman cloisters, high, pointed, and related to Saracenic architecture, are very beautiful. The illuminated missals in the library are magnificent, and wonderfully preserved, while the picture gallery has good examples of the Neopolitan school of painting in the seventeenth and eighteenth centuries. This convent is now a public school. It was here, in this lovely spot, that we first heard of Padula; admiring some illuminated missals of the eleventh or twelfth century, we asked what was their origin, and were told the following story:—In about 1860 a learned archivist from the convent went down to market in La Cava to buy some cheese. He chose a piece of his favourite " Mozzarella," and it was handed to him wrapped up in a sheet of an early illuminated missal. Inquiring where it had come from, he learnt that the farmer wrapped up all his eggs, cheese, and butter in these papers, which he had found lying about in the library of the empty Certosa di Padula. The archivist was able to buy the two remaining cartloads, and these exquisite fragments, as fine as any things of their kind in Italy, now repose in the library at La Cava. Even this curious story, however, did not succeed in focusing attention upon Padula, and it was only a few years ago that the monastery, together with most ancient buildings in the peninsula, was declared a national monument.

Before the dawn of the Steel Age in Europe the traveller was necessarily a man of leisure; all places were equally difficult to reach, all roads were equally bad. Up to 1830 any traveller who succeeded in getting so far as Naples would be sure to persevere, venturing through the beautiful but dangerous landscape—a landscape swarming with brigands as well as with the minor plagues of the South—to inspect the famous Certosa di Padula, as certainly as he would visit Pompeii, Pæstum, and the other classical ruins in the Neapolitan kingdom.

But the advent of the railway in Italy has altered all this, making Padula seem more distant than it was a hundred years ago, altering, too, the position and taste of the traveller. The roads to Padula are broken down, the railway journey is interminable, and the villages round it have been shattered by wars and earthquakes.

The American steel king is no man of leisure.

La Certosa di Padula

He visits Pæstum, about forty miles from Padula, in his steel torpedo car, draws a hasty comparison between Greece and the grandeur that is Chicago, and charges home again—at eighty miles an hour —to Naples. Steel kings, trained to the worship of elephantiasis, should prefer vastness to proportion, Padula to Pæstum: but Pæstum is a Paying Concern, and Delivers the Goods. The eye judges size by the human form, roughly dividing the height of a building by the stature of a man; therefore photographs of the Paying Concern are carefully circulated, with the doll-like temples rising up immense, a child or dwarf in the foreground, much as one of the more manikin-like of European kings is continually photographed, striking his breast in a Louis XIV. manner, with a dwarf placed in the offing. This gives scale. The monarch becomes a vast military figure, bristling moustache — ferocious expression. The temples soar to heaven. The steel king, while he is attracted to Pæstum by the prospect of seeing an earlier sky-scraper, is, on arrival, agreeably surprised by the superior vastness of his office at home. Thus, put in good humour, he spends half-an-hour visiting the temples, tips all the custodians (who are kept out of the way when the photographer comes round), buys a huge quantity of picture-postcards at exorbitant prices, and then dashes back to Naples, leaving a trail of white dust a mile long behind him. In any

Discursions

case the Certosa di Padula would be too highly-seasoned a dish for his dyspeptic digestion. He prefers the Art of Phidias. Pæstum is—or was once—Greek. In its present condition its interest is purely historical. It is no more related to its former beauty than would be the skeleton of Helen of Troy to hers. Like our own cenotaph, it is not a triumph of good or of bad taste, but simply a triumph of no taste at all. It does not exist except as a picturesque ruin, like the unfinished hotel in Piccadilly. Meanwhile the marbles—and the skilful blending of their colours was once the real beauty of Pæstum—now blush unseen, unlooked for, in Padula, Caserta, and a hundred deserted palaces.

It remains a curious commentary on that ill-balanced and ever-changing quality known as "good taste" that while the ruins of Greek temples, the fragments of decadent Greek statues are still admired dotingly, the paintings of Guido Reni and Carlo Dolci, which belong to the same taste, and indeed helped to form it, are still neglected and despised.

Seventy - five miles south - east of Naples the Certosa di Padula lies lost and forgotten, unvisited alike by Italians and foreigners. In the last eighty years probably not more than ten Englishmen have visited it altogether. The guide-books enter into this conspiracy of silence, either not mentioning it at all or referring to the "once famous but now completely ruined Carthusian monastery." All the information we could glean about it in the surrounding towns, was that it had been the largest and most elaborate convent in Italy; that it was supposed to have been ruined by the French in that curious campaign when Massena commanded the French, before Murat became King of Naples —during that same decade when Nelson suddenly took to the land, much to the surprise of the French—as the whale is supposed to have done before him—and proved himself a true amphibian —quite as much at home on land as on sea. In spite of Nelson's genius, however, this particular campaign reflected little but military credit upon our nation. We had queer friends in those days. The brigands and lazzaroni, at that time about ten per cent. of the nation (there were forty thousand lazzaroni in Naples alone), were the only people who really wished to retain their King, Ferdinand IV., afterwards—his only paradox— Ferdinand I. This monarch was the " Re Nasone," so called because of the full Bourbon development of his profile, and grandfather of our former hero, Bomba. He was practically one of themselves, completely uneducated, speaking the lazzaroni dialect, swearing, eating macaroni with his fingers!

In 1780, before any new political ideas had begun to break through the exquisite veneer of the eighteenth century, William Beckford gives us this description of the monarch :

Discursions

" . . . I was obliged to check my impatience and hurry to the Palace in form and gala. A courtly mob had got thither upon the same errand, daubed over with lace and most notably be-periwigged. Nothing but bows and salutations were going forward on the staircase, one of the largest I ever beheld, and which a multitude of prelates and friars were ascending with awkward pomposity. I jostled along to the presence chamber, where his Majesty was dining alone in a circular enclosure of fine clothes and smirking faces. The moment he had finished, twenty long necks were poked forth, and it was a glorious struggle amongst some of the most decorated who first should kiss his hand, the great business of the day. Everybody pressed forward to the best of their abilities. His Majesty seemed to eye nothing but the end of his nose, which is doubtless a capital object.

" Though people have imagined him a weak monarch, I beg leave to differ in opinion, since he has the boldness to prolong his childhood and be happy, in spite of years and conviction. Give him a boar to stab, and a pigeon to shoot at, a battledore or an angling rod, and he is better contented than Solomon in all his glory, and will never discover, like that sapient sovereign, that all is vanity and vexation of spirit."

But in the nineteen years that ensued, the King had managed to outrage the feelings of even his most devoted followers, and the younger aristocratic generation had become influenced in their ideas by the French Revolution.

The brigands and lazzaroni, however, still remained loyal to their King, for they realised that if Naples had a civilised ruler, their day would be over. Sworn reactionaries, they resented violently the French attempts to open schools, make roads, and abolish the Inquisition. Becoming more and more furious at the success of the French arms, they accused the local nobility and educated class of being Jacobins and revolutionaries. A reign of terror ensued, there being a series of frightful massacres. Madame Giglioli, in *Naples in 1799*, gives us an excellent and typical example of the behaviour of the King's partisans :

" In his magnificent palace in the Piazza of San Giovanni Maggiore lived Ascanio Filomarino, Duke della Torre, together with his aged mother, his wife, a young grown-up son and other younger children, and his brother Clemente. The duke was a mathematician and geologist, whose Vesuvian museum, cabinets of valuable instruments and other scientific collections were the admiration of cultured foreigners. He was personally attached to the King and even to the Bourbon Government, and was particularly averse to the novelties of the day. He had proposed to follow the King to Sicily, but had been refused permission ; perhaps he was too cultured and learned a man to be thought safe company for the royal family. 'All good people at that time,' his son tells us (in his memoirs), 'shut up in their own houses, without a guide, without advice, discussed, consulted and deliberated in family council upon the grave events that were drawing fatally near.' Such a family council had been held on the night of 18th January in the Filomarino Palace, and it had been decided that the duke and his sons at any rate had better leave the capital and retire for a time to Sorrento. The idea had been maturing some little time, and the duke had recently made an extra provision of ready money, to the amount of eighteen thousand ducats, which was now in the house.

" ' But alas !' " (I quote the son's words) " 'time was not given us . . . the Piazza of San Giovanni Maggiore is beginning to fill with people on the look-out for mischief. The order was given to shut the palace. The crowd increases, the sedition is evident ; they insist on the opening of the big door. My grandmother opposes this, and also my mother ; my father orders the door to be thrown open ; in a moment the house fills with a crowd of lazzaroni. . . .'

". . . The mob next began to try to break in the doors of the apartments, beginning with that of the duke on the first floor, where were all his valuable collections and the money brought together for the projected flight to Sorrento. Anger gave him greater courage, and he began vehemently reproaching them, declaring that so far from looking for Jacobins they were intent only on robbing and spoiling. At this the mob, leaving for the moment the first floor, surged up the stairs, and broke into the upper apartment, where the terrified family were gathered together. They were led by a barber of the Molo Piccolo, familiar no doubt with the palace and its rich appointments, as barbers were with the house of the rich aristocracy in those days of elaborate toilettes, wigs, and powder. While one party seized the unhappy duke, another broke into the rooms of Clemente Filomarino, who on this very morning had made more than one attempt to destroy himself, and had at last been put to bed by force.

"In a moment the two unhappy brothers were whirled away down and out of the house by the furious mob. The young Filomarino bounded after them half-way down the stairs, but was stopped and obliged to return. After hours of agonised suspense the family, by means of secret heavy bribes to certain of the mob, were able to leave the palace on condition of their taking nothing with them, and that night they took refuge in a monastery. It was not for some days that they knew that the duke and his brother, dragged with insults and blows to the Marinella, had there been bound upon chairs and shot by the lazzari, and their dead bodies burned in tar barrels on two great bonfires.

"The son, whom the lazzari repented of not

having taken and shot also, and whom they traced
to the monastery, spent that night concealed in the
family vault, among the coffins of his forefathers,
but he was so stupefied by the accumulated suffering
of the day that the place had no horror for him."[1]

In the country districts, as in the towns, everything was in a state of pandemonium, the brigands
in rustic localities playing the part of the lazzaroni
in the urban. That part of the population not
actively engaged in massacring, or passively in
being massacred, accused the brigands and their
friends of being in the pay of the English
Government—an accusation never actually proved.

King Ferdinand had fled from Naples, in the
congenial company of his Queen, Lady Hamilton
and Lord Nelson, thereby giving his loyal subjects,
the lazzaroni, a long-sought opportunity of sacking
his palace. No doubt they especially treasured the
many relics they took from it. Meanwhile their
ruler was busy diverting himself in his own way
at Palermo. Hugh Elliot, the British ambassador
there, describes him — in his journal — "as immensely enjoying this period of his life ; above all
rejoicing with strange gesticulations and stranger
words when from some safe place he watched the
artillery practice from the opposite shores : clapping

---

[1] Madame Giglioli throws out the illuminating suggestion that barbers bore an especial grudge toward those suspected of revolutionary
sympathies because they were the first to adopt the new fashion
of cutting the hair short and discarding wigs ! Is this not another
argument against "shingling"?

La Certosa di Padula

his hands with glee when a shot struck some miserable vessel hugging the coast, and apparently perfectly unmindful of the fact that such boats on either side of the strait were manned by his own subjects and countrymen."

During Murat's reign in Naples the roads were made as good and as safe as any in Europe; the Neapolitan debt, which had been steadily increasing under Ferdinand, was completely paid off; education prospered; the lazzaroni actually did some work; Naples became a seat of culture and learning, and the royal palaces were thoroughly cleaned, renovated, and splendidly refurnished. The bandits were the only sufferers. When, after the victory of the Allies, the legitimate king arrived back in an English vessel from his enforced exile in Sicily, the lazzaroni sent him an address of welcome, with an official spokesman in costume. Lady Morgan, in her journal of 1820, describes the triumphant progress of Ferdinand through his dominions, observing, rather dramatically, that the brigands "washed their blood-stained hands to fling a flower in his filthy passage." They then went home to enjoy a forty years' boom in their trade.

Before arriving at his palace of Portici, from the English man-of-war that carried him there, Ferdinand sent on his eldest son, Francis, to see if the palaces were in order, and told him to come back and report on them. This innocent youth, enchanted with Murat's improvements and splendour, ran back to his father, exclaiming with great delight, in front of the whole Court: "Oh! Papa mio! If you had only stayed away another ten years!"

The train journey to Padula being impossible, we had to hire a motor-car, a lengthy and quarrelsome proceeding, the chauffeurs being disappointed or retired brigands, more successful in their new calling. Leaving behind us the almost Chinese landscape of Amalfi and Maiori, with its blue seas, orange-groves, lemon woods, caves, grottos, turrets, towering crags and flying buttresses of limestone rock, we soon reached Salerno, last outpost of civilisation, where stands the great cathedral built by Robert Guiscard, and beyond it the plain that leads to Pæstum. Flat, marshy land is this, full of the feathery asphodel and wild marigold, while herds of malarious wild buffaloes wander about, too weak to notice strangers. These animals form a real reservoir of malaria. The young anopheles mosquito, rising from the marshes through the faint scent of asphodel on the first fine day of the year, has only, out of youthful high spirits, to sting one of these stupid-looking animals round the eye, ear, or some other soft place, to develop the disease itself and hand it on, a fortnight later, to any human being who happens to be in the vicinity. The road soon branches off from the thoroughfare to Pæstum, in the direction of Eboli, a pleasant-looking but rather unhealthy town at the foot of the mountains, formerly the haunt of the most notorious brigands in the Kingdom of the Two Sicilies. My grandfather's guide-book, published in 1853, has the following instructive note in it :—

"The spot where our countryman Mr Hunt and his wife were murdered about twenty-five years ago is on the road to Eboli. They had slept at that town, and his servant had placed on a table near the window the contents of Mr Hunt's dressing-case, which were mounted in silver. A girl belonging to the inn saw them, and spread the report that an English 'Milor,' carrying with him enormous treasures, was going to Pæstum. Eighteen men immediately set out from Eboli, to intercept this reputed spoil. Mr and Mrs Hunt took their luncheon in the Temples, and were returning in an open *calèche* when they were stopped about a mile from the town. They at once surrendered their money and watches; the brigands then demanded '*Il tesoro*,' and Mr Hunt having no idea that they meant the contents of his dressing-case, assured them that he had given up everything. They threatened to shoot him if he persisted in concealing '*Il tesoro*'; upon which he told them that they dared not fire upon an Englishman. Two of them instantly fired; one ball mortally wounded Mr Hunt, the other his wife. The brigands fled to the mountains, and the Government were anxious to hush up the affair ;

Discursions

but the English and Russian Ministers[1] insisted on a judicial investigation, the result of which was that seventeen out of the eighteen robbers were identified by a shepherd boy who witnessed the whole affair while concealed in a thicket. These men were executed, and the eighteenth confessed on his death-bed."

From Eboli onward, the journey becomes increasingly beautiful; the valleys are full of asphodel and marigold, narcissus and jonquil spring up from the level lawns of grass on each side of the narrow streams, and over all these float the magenta or rose-pink blossoms of Judas- and Upas-trees. The fantastic landscape, of enormous dimensions, is dominated by Monte Alburno, that mountain beloved of Virgil, the cracked and riven outline of which shows like a broken knife-edge against the vibrating blue of the sky. It is not possible to imagine the other side of this giant mountain, for it seems as if that nearest to us had been cut in cardboard and painted to resemble a hill, so that the other side would be hollow, unpainted and dusty, a shelter perhaps for theatrical ogres or stage thunder. The long summit looks as though pieces had been cut out of it by a child with a pair of scissors, but the bare granite surface is coolly radiant as ice on this hot day, showing every

[1] It is a comment on modern life, that now, under similar circumstances, it is more probable that the Russian Minister would insist on some share of the proceeds.

colour embraced in the predominant blue or purple of its shadows. Far down below sings that Greek stream, the Tanager, and to echo it lies the lovely Valle di Diano, a volcanic valley with the usual array of craters and hot streams, and rivers that run under ground for a mile or two. Through the haze that hangs over this vast view, small hills rise up so regular in shape that they appear to be deep blue pyramids.

Everywhere the flowers are miraculous in their quality and profusion, drifts of asphodel and marigold, orchids and roses, narcissus and anemone of every colour, with flowering bushes and trees leaning over them. It is difficult to think of the English and French troops fighting out their dreary old quarrels, that had already lasted four hundred years too long, in this very strange landscape, only a century ago. How many men were killed and wounded, how many died of malaria, typhoid and other fevers?

Some of the grey houses are in ruins, for the earthquakes in this district are very severe, that of 1857 killing twenty thousand people.

Very few living things are to be seen in this landscape: a shepherd boy—a boy of about fourteen or fifteen, dressed in goatskins, just as his ancestors were one thousand or two thousand years ago—an old farmer, and a few loud-barking dogs. The villages seem empty. Houses are large, solid, built of grey stone. We see a few towns on the hill-sides, quite large towns with gaily-painted, stout - built houses. The towns become more plentiful, and then, suddenly, a great gateway, unattached to any road, appears out of the plain, and beyond it an enormous, low building, vast as a town, swelling out of the vegetation round it, as if it, too, were part of the soil. Here in this distant, unvisited, poverty-stricken plain, unwept by the world, with only a slight mournful "keening" from Baedeker, is a monument of the first order, the discovery of a building as romantic and remote as any that could be encountered in the central forest of Brazil.

The outside wall stretches for a mile, then comes a fine entrance, facing in the direction away from Naples, with a paved court through it. In this first court is the real façade of the Certosa, built of a lovely, soft yellow stone, resembling more nearly the buildings of Vanbrugh than those of San Felice, Vanvitelli or other Neapolitan architects. No sign is here of crumbling plaster or bright paint, but a stout-built front akin to Blenheim or Castle Howard. As a stage effect, it is better lighted than its English cousins, no mists or heavy outlines, but strong hard effects; masks peer at you from the walls, and the ascending saints posture and grimace against the unvarying blue stage-cloth of the background. Through the centre, pillared portico is seen a Bibbiena - like vista of two cloisters, the nearer in the same style,

THE CERTOSA OF PADULA

GREAT COURT OF CERTOSA OF PADULA

La Certosa di Padula

of the same period (about 1720) as the façade, the further one simpler, and of later date, but even more impressive in size, the four sides of the court making a walk of a kilometre. So vast is this building that, during the war, six thousand Austrian prisoners were quartered in it—but there is no sign of the guide-book's "complete ruin." It is not destroyed, it is only empty, with a few smashed pieces of furniture, a few pictures gone to Paris with Murat, and some dislodged plaster-work.

The Certosa di Padula, like the Escurial, is dedicated to San Lorenzo, and, like that palace-monastery, is built on the plan, in the shape, of the Saint's Gridiron. This morbid Spanish influence is felt in the whole building, though it is the influence of southern and not of northern Spain. In the first cloister are the chapel, the strangers' chapel, and the guest-rooms. All these have exquisite gilded plaster-work, quite unspoilt. The chapel is a fine building, the usual Carthusian one, with a great wealth of marble, mostly from Pæstum, decorated with the gridiron and the emblem of the Carthusian Order. There is also some beautiful furniture in it, chairs, tables, and candlesticks. Indeed, the monks here appear to have evolved a special style of inlaid furniture. In the sacristy was a whole lumber-room of chairs, tables, balusters and gilded junk. Out of this first court lead several smaller ones, some showing traces of twelfth-century work. Each of them has a delightful fountain, unlike any to be seen elsewhere in Italy, very rich, original, and imaginative in conception.

The second court, enormous in scale, is simple and refined work of about 1760. Opening out of it are the cells or, rather, private suites of the brothers. Each monk here had a large bedroom, a very big sitting-room, a loggia'd garden in proportion to the room, and a private fountain and vista. Indeed a fountain seems to have been the equivalent of a bathroom in a modern hotel — "complete with fountain, vista, and every modern convenience." The Abbot's apartments and garden were of the most magnificent, and one cannot imagine a more delightful home. Since the Carthusian Order was a noble one, the monks were allowed servants, and their life in Padula, surely, cannot have been too Spartan a one.

In this cloister, upstairs, is the library—that magnificent library from which came the illuminated missals at La Cava. The paintings, that were framed in the plaster-work of the walls, have gone to Paris, but there are still numberless books in the unguarded and unkept shelves.

Beyond this court, in the garden outside, is perhaps the most remarkable feature of this whole building, itself one of the greatest Baroque monuments in Italy. Here is the entrance from the Naples road. The tired traveller would see what looked like an enormous belvedere, a temple with a rounded cupola, towering in the distance.

La Certosa di Padula

Arriving, entering it, he would find no temple, but a flying double-staircase, a conjuring trick in rich golden stone. With large windows opening into the azure emptiness of the sky, this cupola contains a staircase more developed and more strange than any of its trapeze-like cousins in Naples. After the most astonishing convolutions and serpentine windings, travellers find themselves landed breathless at a huge door above.

Let us imagine the scene. Two young bewigged Neapolitan grandees, on their annual visit to their unfortunate estates in Calabria, ride through the baked summer landscape. Leaving their attendants to look after themselves, they dismount wearily and enter this ice-cool temple. They mount the stairs, one taking one staircase, one the other — a simple affair. But this staircase, like the fabulous roc, would lift them bodily in the air, whirl them up and down, show each to the other for one brief moment, circle them round again, shake them, entangle them again for a second, separate them, catch them in a vortex of stone, peering masks, and slashes of blue sky, until it finally drops them, breathless and bewildered, at the Sacred Door above, where a meek brother waits to take them by the hand, and lead them through long corridors to their bedrooms, a mile or so away! Thus, too, the later Roman Emperors received ambassadors of barbarous States, on a throne, at the top of a floating staircase, so high and imposing that the poor ambassador could find no breath or pride with which to answer the Emperor's questions for a full half-hour.

As we turned to leave the monastery, with deep regret, a strange thing happened. We were led to write our names in an empty visitors' book. I proffered the custodian the usual tip. He refused it politely and asked me to give it to the man who had opened the doors. This tall and dignified individual looked at the note in wonder, and then handed it back. Some breath of holiness, some lingering odour of sanctity, must still haunt this empty place.

Part II

Cities of the Phœnix

i

Round Etna

CATANIA is, without doubt, a city to visit —but not to stay in. When once you have seen it, and, in spite of the noise and obvious squalor, have felt its attraction, moments arrive in your life when you feel compelled to return there; but never allow yourself to be tempted to remain in the city. There is a quality of horror about these large, hot, draughty, dirty, empty, noisy hotels that is lacking in far dirtier and more palpably unpleasant ones.

Used as I am to the thoughtfulness of Southern Italian and Sicilian hotel-keepers, the dead rat deposited, apparently as a tribute, on the mat by my bedroom door, was more than I could for long endure. There it was, laid-out in state, under the high glass roof of the corridor, in all its funeral pomp; and as, bolted within my room, I lay awake, haunted by thoughts of the silent sentinel outside, the unwelcome memory of many old acquaintances in the insect, reptile, and rodent world came back to me. There were the rats in the trenches— plump brutes that dropped from the branches of shattered trees into the muddy pools below with a fat sound of splashing, as they weltered and wallowed in the mud. There were, too, those beetles in the dining - room of the small inn at Monte Cassino, where we were once stranded for the night, unable to obtain accommodation at the Monastery because so many dignitaries of the Church were then making their Easter retreat— beetles that at the slightest movement dropped in showers from wall and curtain on to the tables and floor below. Even worse was the recollection of my tent in the camp at Marlowe. Situated in a large, flat, grass field on the top of a hill, bounded by hanging wood, no English scene could have been more beautiful, more typical of its county; but a plague of earwigs, perhaps the most horrible of English pests, hung over us like a cloud, and at night, if the canvas were ever so slightly touched, would fall squirming on to bed and floor. There was that earwig which had attacked me in my bath at Weston. Suddenly looking round, I saw it parting the waters with a vigorous side-stroke, and making for my big toe. A terrific and lengthy battle ensued. Then there was my old friend the scorpion, who waxes fat on the bones of saints and holy men in the chapel at Montegufoni. Scorpions are not common in Tuscany, but this one has thrived for many years, possibly protected by the patron saint upon whom he feeds. A horrid dragon he is, as he crouches on the wall, guarding the numerous cases of glass and gilded wood, in which lie revealed the parchment-coloured relics, tied up with coquettish bows of salmon - pink ribbon, with an occasional orange-flower placed here and there, to awaken in these dry, meagre bones memories of the flesh that once adhered to them, but yet a guardian preferable to that one now sleeping his last sleep without. Finally I thought again of the snake, which I saw on a fine August morning, clambering up the garden-steps of the hotel where I am now writing into what, considering the discomfort of the chairs that grace it, is somewhat euphemistically known as "the lounge." This snake was very impressive, not very large, but a dowager obviously, and boasting of I know not how many quarterings; so heraldic, so viperous was it, that anywhere it would have passed as the model for the Sforza coat-of-arms; and the Sforzas, in truth, sprang from the same soil. "Only something come in from the lake," the porter reassured me, as he disposed of its mangled corpse; but I have never yet met reptile or insect that failed to rouse my loathing, and I lay in bed praying for the day of Wells' Utopia, when none of such things would be permitted to exist, except as caged specimens of the evils that men had for many millions of years borne willingly, making no concerted effort to destroy, content with attempting the extermination of their own kind.

Alas, even a dead rat may affect human happiness more than one would, at first, deem possible.

Discursions

In order to avoid other encounters of this kind I decided to move on, ten miles or so, to Acireale. Here, it was stated, was a new and comfortable hotel in a little-frequented city on the beautiful slopes of Etna. As a matter of strict accuracy the hotel was an old one, that for some reason or other had remained empty for twenty years, but its renovation was sufficiently recent for the paint on the wall to be still damp, and the rooms quite unheated. January nights are cold everywhere, even in Sicily, and as a result I caught a chill and influenza, and was ill for some time.

That hotel, an immense building on the high road, near the railway, will ever remain a mystery. If you sleep on the side of the street, the passing railway engine almost puts its funnel in at your window and runs under the bed; on the other side is a gloomy but rather beautiful view of Etna. The bedrooms are few—about thirty—but lofty. The bathrooms are many, but with no hope of water. The sitting-rooms are of immense size; the dining-room, with its high, vaulted ceiling, is a really beautiful room, large enough to seat four or five hundred people. Its actual owner was an immensely rich and eccentric Sicilian nobleman, who paid for everything, and it was run by a charming, fat Sicilian hotel-keeper. But were this hotel everything that was promised of it, who except an occasional visitor like myself would wish to stay in—or come to—such a town? The

Round Etna

prospectus of the hotel read like one of Mr Lloyd George's speeches—a fact that should, perhaps, have warned us. We were promised orange-groves, gardens of deliciously - smelling flowers, constant - hot - water, shower - baths, an American bar, two tennis-courts, and, speaking generally, 9d. for 4d. ; but all these things were but mirages, the figments of the Sicilian Marchese's fervent imagination, the product of my fat friend's realistic literary style. For the non-existence of the tennis-courts we were, however, duly grateful, because those people who come to the slopes of Etna from England and America in order to play tennis or golf must be very unpleasant mental - defectives, and ones, too, who usually evince a passion for general conversation.

There was on this occasion little danger of casual conversation, since we were the first and only guests in the establishment. Being therefore regarded as somewhat in the nature of mascots, we were invited by our genial manager to attend the opening ceremony of his new hotel, which was to be blessed publicly by the Bishop of Acireale at three o'clock the following afternoon. The host, I regret to write, did not altogether believe in the efficacy of this benediction, but he told me that the people of the town—a city of sixty thousand souls, full of the prosperous and well-educated as well as of poor illiterates—were so deeply religious that, unless the hotel received the

Discursions

Episcopal blessing, not one of them would enter its doors.

A crowd of managers, secretaries, and local magnates, all clad solemnly in frock-coats, was waiting in the hall, when punctually at two-fifty-five a motor-car (provided by the hotel) drew up at the door. Its large panes of glass revealed the Bishop within, in the full glory of robes, mitre, and crook. Immediately the crowd dashed to the door, each member of it hoping to be the first to kiss the ring. The ceremony then began, about four hundred guests being present. The Bishop, a very solemn figure, walked slowly, followed by the crowd, through the corridors, bed-rooms, and high, vaulted sitting-rooms, while an acolyte in front scattered holy water, or occasionally himself would lift two fingers in the gesture of benediction. We then all hurried downstairs to the dining-room, to engage in an orgy of ices and sweet champagne, for in Sicily men—even bishops—do not scorn an ice as they do in Northern countries. A mandolin band, meanwhile, treated us to selections from *Carmen* and *Rigoletto*; but the Bishop, in order not to spoil too much the general enjoyment by his austere presence, soon swept out to the strains of the March in *Aida*—music very appropriate to him, as he strode out in his mitre, which conjured up visions of the high priests of Egypt. The music now changed; Neapolitan songs and rather

Photograph : Alinari

CATANIA : THE CATHEDRAL.

Round Etna

decadent rag-time became the order of the evening, and dancing lasted for some hours.

It must be admitted that, in January, Acireale is an unpleasant place. There is always something a little irritating about a town that is near but not on the sea, nor yet high enough above it, as for example is Ravello, to make the sin of omission excusable. Nor here has the sea receded, as at Ravenna; so that no extenuating circumstance can be pleaded on behalf of its citizens, who must be a dull, unimaginative body; while, owing to the buildings and general lay-out of the town, it is difficult even to obtain a view of the blue waters. Worse still, the town is situated too near Etna, the other chief feature of the landscape, to obtain a view of it, such as you get from places as far removed as Taormina and Syracuse, while the smoke from the craters drifts over the town, blotting out the sunshine that makes the days warm even in January, causing constant showers of rain, and giving the place temporarily the atmosphere of Sheffield or the Five Towns. Etna is an object of such beauty that, while so near the mountain, to be deprived of the view of it is a real misfortune. From Taormina it dominates the landscape absolutely, yet has an idyllic pastoral beauty; the long gradual slope seems to fill the horizon, the smoke being like a white cloud reflecting and reversing its snow-cap in the sky above, contradicting the usual order of pool and tree, lake and hill.

Discursions

From Syracuse it floats far off, and even more beautiful, high above the flat landscape and peacock-winged sea. From here it seems all snow, like a large snow mound, or the icy tent of some Arctic god, Woden or Thor, who must have marched hither with the Northern armies. From Catania it is more impressive, perhaps less lovely, because its colour is black—a huge black giant, the old Cyclops, who will soon crush the town by hurling down on it immense rocks. But from Acireale you can see little of it, though at night you could hear the subterranean thunder. And at the time of which I am writing there was a queer feeling in the air: the great eruption which took place a few months later was already, no doubt, being prepared below; and after dark, when the shrill-ing of the bells and hoarse voices of the men driving their mules over the almost impassable roads had died down, the air was resonant with distant roaring—bellowing almost—and Etna would be revealed crowned with such fire as had not been seen for many decades. We comforted our-selves by reflecting that usually while a volcano is very active there is less danger of sudden explosion; but we could not help picturing the scenes if an eruption should take place. The country lanes at this time of year hardly exist at all, the streets and roads of the town were as foul as those of towns in England two hundred years ago. These would be utterly choked and blocked

Round Etna

by the rush of fugitives, rough men at any time
and now mad with fear, from the slopes of Etna,
one of the most thickly-populated districts in the
world. They would come down in this direction,
seeking the sea as a means of escape. They
would be in a panic, have no discipline. Theft
and murder would be common among them, and
the foreigner caught in such a sudden orgy of
terror would have little chance. And all the time
the red snakes of the lava would be hissing, un-
coiling down the mountain, like huge dragons,
swallowing up whole orchards, gardens, and even
towns. The only man who would be able to stay
the terror in any degree (and dreadful his responsibility!) would be the Bishop. The churches would
be full of the calmer part of the population kneeling
to pray, refusing to leave even though the roof was
breaking down under the weight of ashes. The
air outside would be hot, sultry, and full of poisonous
fumes as hell itself—such always is the way of
eruptions, and such was it six months later—but
in that January we thought the vision merely our
evil-imaginings, the result of an over-taut nervous
system—just as we treated the nightmare of a
world-war when it sometimes crept into our mind
in the spring and early summer of 1914.

As a town Acireale is, in January at any rate,
a disappointment. The opera (at which Madame
Albani sang during the opening tour of her career)
was not yet open. The streets were hardly possible

L   161

to walk in, while to go out into the country was, obviously, an impossibility. And the whole place was dreadfully, terribly smelly. Even as regards architecture the town, though excessively strange, belied our hopes. Like most cities in the neighbourhood, it had been destroyed by the exceptionally severe earthquake of 1693. This, no doubt, overwhelmed a number of beautiful buildings here too, for nowhere else in the world are to be found so many noble examples of different styles placed near together as in Sicily. In the other parts of the island, where earthquakes are comparatively rare and mild, Greek temples, Saracenic mosques, Byzantine cathedrals, Norman castles, Gothic and Renaissance palaces, Baroque, Rococo and Empire buildings, jostle one another in the street in a pleasing, astonishing manner. But in Acireale these relics of former civilisation have either been shaken down, or lie under their coats of lava, one above the other in layers, petrified but patient, waiting for their living sister to join them, and a new one to be born in her stead.

Though this total destruction of the city must have meant the loss of most interesting monuments, it yet gave to a town rich as this one, and in a period of such architectural activity as was the early eighteenth century in Sicily, a great opportunity. Think what Wren would have done if only London had been laid waste by earthquake as well as by fire! But no genius, such as his, was here to seize the chance. Perhaps, too, there was so much building activity in the island, that no architect could be spared from, let us say, Palermo or Syracuse. For the Rococo creations of Palermo are particularly beautiful, recalling the French more than the Italian : Syracuse is different, full of churches and palaces equal to any of the same period, but absolutely Sicilian in style ; while Noto, as well, is a model town of the epoch.

But when the hour for his arrival struck in Acireale, no genius, local or foreign, appeared. On the contrary, far from evoking any new or appropriate style, it seems as if the citizens, tired of earthquakes, were eager merely to bridge over the chasms in the earth with temporary platforms, to hide and cloak the tremors that constantly shook the ground beneath them with hastily-improvised stages and scenery, so as to give the pretence of a certain security and permanence to their lives. They wanted their dwellings to have just enough of the appearance of a town to make them feel safe from the ravages of the giant who continually threatened them, tall enough, if possible, to blot out his presence. They did not want solidity, which had been proved useless, but a series of thin-built palaces and churches, as easily put up, as easily shaken down, as the paper houses of Japan. On the other hand they insisted upon, at any rate, the semblance of a background to their lives, and were not content with mud huts and rag buildings, as is now the population of the large city of Messina. To give themselves this background, then, they built their façades, and on them hung masks; and above these balanced wide balconies with bow-like railings. And such masks as these were never before seen, masks whose quality of amusement, here apparently the only aim, was derived solely from the physical suffering and degraded physique of a slum population; but this trait amused each century in turn except the nineteenth and, let us hope, the twentieth. Such brutalised masks and debased grimaces are merely a fantasia based upon the crowd in these cities—crowds among which, in spite of the usually fine development of the Sicilians, a splendid-looking race, there was always a large proportion of dwarfs, hunchbacks, and other monstrosities, filling the market-place with cackling and idiot laughter. Yet in spite of the coarseness of these masks and buildings, there is something impressive about them, something of the primitive quality to be found in the totem-poles of Canada. There is also, obviously, to be felt in them the influence of the long Spanish Domination, a suggestion of a harder people—perhaps of bull-fight and Inquisition. . . ? And this Spanish influence, while it accounts for the air of cruelty, at the same time is the only one that gives the buildings any artistic value, for in spite of shortcomings, they have the vitality and strict conventions, the rhythm and surprising dissonances of popular Spanish music.

With the streets and squares thus hastily thrown up, like the scenery of an improvised theatre, the life of the town could continue as before. In the daytime an orator could address the market-place with bold words and gestures from one of the balconies, while the masks below reflected the democratic feelings of surprise, horror, and laughter. At night, however, the masks would be hidden, and the balconies would become floating rafts in the air, from which cool music could drip down into the hot ways below, or barges, moored high among the fresh play of the young winds, from which for once, reversing the usual order, the ladies masked by darkness would serenade the men waiting below, or, themselves silent, watch the life flowing beneath them and hear the snarling voices and deep braying of the piazzas carried up by eddies of warm flower-scented air.

There is, however, one church that points to the purer style and possible beauty which would have existed in Acireale if only the earth had kept quiet as in other lands. The Church of San Sebastiano is a noble and refined work of art. The large stone front, with a dignity and solidity that are lightened by the play of a whimsical and original mind, presents a great contrast to everything round it. The wide paved platform before its portals, at the top of a high flight of broad but

Discursions

shallow steps, is railed off by a flight of cupids, whose arms are weighed down by the heavy chains they carry, as if to prevent the rather brutal life of the town, mocked and sneered at by all the leering faces that support window and balcony, from entering to shatter the repose and peace that are to be found within.

.   .   .   .

Before we return to our dead rat in Catania there is one other feature of Acireale which deserves our attention—the painted carts that go lumbering over roads that are like a miniature model of the country-side, with rivers and hills, rocks, lakes, and precipices. Everywhere in Sicily the peasant, when first setting up for himself, spends an incredible proportion of his capital—far more than he would allow himself to lay out on the furnishing of his house or on the equipment of his farm—in buying a decorative harness and a brightly-painted cart. The harness, hung with bells that sound, in the summer weather, cool as a splashing shower of rain, is inset with pieces of mirror that are for ever catching the sun's eye, tracing arabesques of moving light on the walls of houses and gardens, seeming indeed to echo in light the sound of the bells in the air—for at each movement of the mule the bells tinkle and the reflected light on the walls forms a new design. The carts themselves vary in each district. In Palermo, their painted panels are traditional, almost

166

Round Etna

Byzantine in conception, belonging obviously to the same world as Monreale. Of extreme brilliance in colour, they rather resemble the Russian setting for *Coq d'Or* and *Children's Tales*, as these were presented by M. Diaghileff. The scenes depicted on them are usually derived from the poets. Heroic warriors, the memory of whose chivalry and shining armour is now only kept alive by the marionette theatres, are rescuing noble but distressed damsels. For these carts there cannot, in Palermo, be many more than twenty patterns from among which the peasant can choose; going to the painter's he *must* make his choice of one of them, since for him to demand a new and special design would be a breach of convention, etiquette, and almost of respectability, giving the young couple a bad name. But the painting of the cart is not its only beauty, for it boasts also little groups of painted wooden statues — St George and the Dragon, and other such subjects—as well as much fine decorative carving. In Girgenti the carts are different, though the subjects are identical; they are treated less archaistically and are in a more subdued scale of colour; while in Acireale, the peasant, here out of the hands of professional painters, and doing his own decoration, turns to modern life for his inspiration. The various panels of a cart will have portrayed on them "The Triumph of the Allies over Germany and Austria," the seizing of Fiume by d'Annunzio, a view of

167

Discursions

Etna, a toe-in-air ballerina, and an almost Derain-like still-life. But all these different types of carts, in Palermo, Girgenti, Syracuse, and here under the shadow of the volcano, are so entrancing, alive, and unselfconscious, that they probably represent the only satisfactory form of peasant-art that exists in Europe to-day.

ii

Catania

THE life of Catania throbs and shrills noisily outside, for, as befits the second largest, and far the richest, city in Sicily, in clamour it is second to none. The only quiet, placid thing in the hotel is the dead rat still lying by my door. Trams clank, hoot and whistle in the narrow street outside, shutters are barred and unbarred with the rolling of thunder, barrel-organs are already grinding out their accustomed tunes in each piazza in the town, every boy in every street is whistling *Gigoletta,* and an immense lion-like roaring comes out of all the bars and cafés —full even at this early hour. Windows are flung wide open with a loud creaking and banging, and strident voices converse across streets, complicated and intersected by tram-lines, live-wires, telephone and telegraph wires that dodge in and out, here and there, dividing the strip of blue, intense blue sky above into the most complicated and three-dimensional series of patterns that shift every moment as the onlooker moves, like the patterns of a kaleidoscope. But these many voices are strong enough to bridge the general uproar that, redoubled by the formation of the town, is sent crashing back hither by the sudden rise from the lower to the upper city, while the bright flashing sunlight beating down on us seems actually to increase the volume of sound. Then, too, at this moment the Feast of St Agatha, greatest of all Sicilian *festas*, is in preparation. Booths and band-stands are everywhere being hurriedly erected, to the widespread accompaniment of hammering and swearing, while the streets are full of peasants, feeling rather ill-at-ease, watching and listening with calm bullock-like eyes, and clad in the full finery of coloured garments, gold ear-rings and jewellery, for which the Sicilian peasants are famous.

It is a city full of character, and of many surprises. Its situation between Etna and the sea is sufficient, alone, to make it different from other places. But the difference exists more even in the life of the town than in its position and planning. The water here is peculiarly blue, even when stormy, and reflects back with an equal strength the light poured down upon it. Black, bony, tufa-rocks spring out of the sea, echoing the angular grace of the prickly-pears that, alone of the vegetable world, grow on them. Orange and lemon trees flourish in luxuriant little valleys between these rocks that remain naked, yielding never to the softness of the climate or to the vigour of plant-life that marks it. Palms are everywhere

Catania

to be seen on the land, looking healthy and natural objects, not withered and invalid like those in Southern France and Northern Italy. Cactuses of all species, with their fleshy leaves and spiky buds, spring out from every crevice like so many Jacks-in-the-Box, while from here, just outside the boundaries, you can see how the lava has been levelled off, and the city stretched across it, dumped down on it, time after time, with singular courage and pertinacity. Turning a broad curving flank to the sea, the town is divided almost in half by the Via Etnea, a broad straight thoroughfare, the centre of urban life, that stretches for nearly two miles and flashes in the hard light like a dagger dropped between volcano and Mediterranean. The whole place is dominated by the enormous and impressive mountain. The Via Etnea is intersected by several streets, that cut it at right angles; all these end in the sea on one side, and become converted into giant staircases on the other. This at once gives the town an unusual and extraordinarily architectural aspect.

Down in the lower town the bars and cafés are full of young men, whose dress is almost too elegant, though, as they think, thoroughly English, whose cloth - topped patent - leather boots are too shiny, whose suits are too carefully cut. They are either drinking very black coffee or eating ices —orange ices, lemon ices, vanilla ices, cassata Siciliana, coffee ices, chocolate ices, all the subtle varieties of a delectable death—for nowhere are ices as delicious as in Sicilian towns, and in few places is the water supply more suspect than in Catania. The streets are thronged, but there are more women to be seen here walking about than in the country towns, where the old Oriental customs still linger. The Piazza del Duomo is full of prosperous - looking middle - aged men chattering and discussing business, while the hammering now reaches its climax, for a special band will, from this point of vantage, blaze abroad for several days the glory of St Agatha, making this particular celebration of her a matter of talk for many months in the country round. The centre of the piazza holds a large fountain, in which treads heavily an elephant of carved lava, carrying an obelisk of Egyptian granite. This large beast was probably part of the decoration of the ancient arena, and, discovered in the seventeenth century, was placed in this prominent position, and now forms part of the coat-of-arms of the city. The Cathedral, at the side of the square nearest the sea, is an imposing Baroque building, with a rather dull Gothic interior, which contains some fine tombs of the Aragonese family. Built originally in 1091 by King Roger, it was totally destroyed in the earth- quake of 1169 ; but, since its re-erection, the inside of it has somehow escaped being injured by the subsequent numerous shocks. In the little streets behind the Cathedral are the shops of small jewellers, where it is possible to find the coloured amber that is a speciality of Catania. This amber is to be found only in one stream, washed down from the slopes of the volcano. It differs in colour, and is usually shot with another one, as is the opal. Thus there is a straw - coloured variety with a light blue reflection running through it, a dark red one with the same pale blue tone, and numerous other combinations of tone and reflection; but no two pieces are the same. This peculiarly lovely colouring is supposed to be caused by the resin being baked for centuries beneath the hot lava. It is very rare to find big pieces of this amber.

The most interesting buildings in the town are undoubtedly the Church and Monastery of San Niccola, and the Biscari Palace. The former are in the higher part of the city, standing in the midst of a series of regularly - laid - out but extremely dilapidated crescents and squares. The front of the church, which is the largest in the island, was never finished. Giant columns, like those of a Greek temple, rise up, supporting nothing heavier than the airy firmament; while the clouds, which seem but a little way over us, so high are we above the town, draw a distinct tone of blue out of the white stone as their wing-like shadows are cast on it for a moment. Over each of the three doors, flanked by two of these gigantic but uncompleted pillars, are three very

simple but deeply-recessed windows. The steps
are wide and shallow, and the scale of the whole
erection can be guessed from the comparative size
of two children sitting on them, in the photograph.
The church is very cool and very lofty within, but
lacks the dignity of the unfinished façade, which,
though built between 1690 and 1733, must appeal
especially to those who care for Greek remains:
the interior has no particular interest, being
merely bigger in every detail than any other
church; the dome is bigger than other domes, the
tower is taller than any other tower; the organ
has more pipes and is far louder than any other,
and so forth; but as there are no details so
arranged as to give the eye an idea of the general
scale, there is nothing very imposing about it.
There are, of course, those who hold that a very
large building, if perfectly proportioned, should
look no bigger that any other; but if a vast
church is built, simply to impress by its size, and
then looks no larger than a much smaller church
elsewhere, it must surely be a failure?

The convent, placed farther back than the church,
but with its façade parallel to it, is, though of the
same date, in a very contrasting style. The
original plan for the whole body of buildings consisted of a church in the middle, and two courts
on each side. Only two of these were completed,
one behind the other, masked by the façade—
though beyond and behind the church is the

Photograph: Alinari

CATANIA: CHURCH OF S. NICCOLA

beginning of a third court, now transformed into a museum and picture gallery.

The vast mass of grey stucco which composes the two-storeyed front is broken only by one great door, with a large window above, and by the two sets of four or five smaller windows on each side of it, which are divided by pilasters of cut stone with richly-carved capitals. But on the doors and windows depends the effect of the building; the entire decoration of the façade is concentrated on them. They are intensely rich and fantastic, both in detail and general effect, as remote from the usual development of European architecture as the temples in India and Siam; indeed in the way the detail is treated there is something strongly reminiscent of the famous temples of Angkhor. Mr Martin Briggs, to whose valuable book on Lecce we have referred elsewhere, suggests that the architect of the monastery must have seen and been influenced by the Municipio, and other palaces and churches of this date, in Lecce. But it seems to me that they are really too unlike to have been directly influenced by one another, though obviously they show some common ancestry—being both descended, perhaps, from the Plateresque Architecture of Spain. The Municipio and Seminario at Lecce, however much of Spanish influence went to their making, are, in their very bones, Latin; strange as this fantastic edifice at Catania, they are yet, in a sense, classical, always treated in a purely architectural way, and would be recognised anywhere as examples of an Italian style, though of one not previously met with; whereas this Convent of San Niccola suggests Mexico, Majorca or Siam just as much as Italy, and its façade is not treated in an architectural way. On the contrary, the windows and doors are more a specimen of jeweller's work, dealt-with like gems that need a rich setting. In fact this huge edifice, formerly, like the Biscari Palace, one of the sights of Southern Europe, is simply a transcendent example of the style of building to be found at Acireale, lacking the brutality and the coarseness, having the same good qualities magnified and multiplied. What is more, the architect of this convent, and of the Biscari Palace, was a certain Fra Vaccarini, a monk, who also designed the best buildings in Acireale.

Entering the main doorway, with its elaborate decoration, you find an enormous staircase, with marble pillars and frescoes, now a kind of roll-of-honour on which are scrawled in pencil the names of all the dirtiest school children in Catania for the last thirty years; and going up these steps, you can look down from the gallery that runs round it into a large square court, full of palms and cactuses, orange- and lemon-trees, and one which rivals in size that at Padula. Though built toward the middle of the eighteenth century, this court is in the Mudejar style; and peering down into the centre of its square of flowers and falling green shadows, you see a large well under a canopy of green and yellow tiles decorated with arabesque patterns. It is an anachronism, this court, yet one does not feel, as with Walpole's and Pugin's revival of Gothic, that it is a form of fashionable upholstery, comparable to the tasselled cushions and painted lamp-shades of to-day, but rather that this style, ever growing a little weaker, had lingered on in remote places, here to find at length a suitable place for its last febrile flowering.

Before the dissolution of this monastery, its monks were famous for their grand style of living. All the great religious establishments in Sicily were celebrated for their good cooking, and throughout the eighteenth century (which, as in Ireland and other agricultural islands, really continued until about 1850) it was the custom of the local nobility, when they entertained, to order one course for dinner from one convent, one from another. But the most delicious food of all came from the Convento di San Niccola—which may be a reason why the Neapolitan Bourbons, who, like all their race, were noted for their appetites, came here so often and stayed so long. And when the Royal Family paid a visit here, it was their custom to bring with them from Naples for their entertainment the orchestra of the San Carlo theatre. At night the wide-open windows blazed with light, illuminating the cherubs caught in the tendrils of vines, like birds struggling in a thicket, that were carved round them; while the crystal chandeliers in the Royal Apartments scintillated with such effect that they seemed, to the watchers below, to rival the more permanent constellations that appeared from there to be level with them in the sky. The loud strains of the band would pour like a tropical rain-storm on to the green courts and parched blossoms, dashing down the vast flights of steps that led to the lower town like so many water-falls, splashing up even into the open windows of the houses, where the people stood to listen. On the wide staircases themselves the dusty beggars would be cooled by these sounds, which, in spite of their natural laziness, would draw them ever nearer and nearer to the blazing windows at the top of the hill. And then, too, they hoped to catch a sight of their King; a popular figure who played down to his people in a democratic, almost modern, way, favouring continually the more cut-throat element of the population at the expense of the more cultured. And the fat, ogre-like figure of their monarch would appear for an instant at the window, eating macaroni in the same fashion as any Neapolitan lazzarone, and swearing revolt-ingly in Sicilian dialect—tricks that won him the loving appreciation of his subjects, gazing up at him from below.

The Biscari Palace is very similar to this con-vent, though on a much smaller scale. Its windows and doors are also magnificent but unconnected. Visited by all the famous travellers of the eighteenth century, it has been neglected for many years; for since the love of primitive art, which, springing from Byron and Scott, reached its pompous[1] climax in Ruskin, manifested itself, this form of architecture has been in disgrace — has been, so to speak, put in Coventry. Situated on the sea-front, the palace is now dwarfed by docks and iron railway-bridges, looking dusty and forlorn as Cinderella. It consists of a low, long pavilion of two storeys, with an imposing outside staircase, and a fine courtyard which is entered from the street behind, and not from the front of the palace. Goethe came here, during his visit to Sicily, in order to see the Prince's famous collection of antique works of art, which is still housed here, though the family have moved into a newer residence.

Besides these two, there are numerous less important examples of Fra Vaccarini's work in the town, another unusual feature of which is the number of rococo churches, built with curving pillared façades and curving steps in line with them. These very simple churches, beautifully planned, depending for their effect solely on their grace of line and freedom from unnecessary ornament, contrast forcibly with the elaborate detail of their neighbours.

[1] Typists often have their inspirations, and the young lady who transcribed this word rendered it "pom-pom," a very adequate description. She told me she had read all Ruskin's works.

Discursions

But, in spite of its architectural achievement, Catania remains more remarkable for its life and general atmosphere. Walking down from San Niccola, in a narrow street of tall houses, lofty churches, and doorways that revealed vistas of garden wall and grey cloister, we were surprised, on looking up at the sky, to see suddenly, far off, a ship in full sail above the houses. There could be no doubt about it; the vessel was a feature of the sky rather than of the sea. This peculiar perspective of its own, due to the sharp rise and fall of the ground, gives the city at once an air that is strange and unearthly. It is the sort of thing that would not be tolerated in England. Were I, for instance, to begin a poem with the lines

> " I see a ship above the houses ;
> Over my head it sails away,"

those critics, the working of whose minds it is my hobby to unravel, would, if I am not mistaken, dismiss them as the raving of a lunatic. Yet here it is a statement of sober fact.

Slightly startled by this apparition in the blue dome above us, we turned the corner, only to be confronted by a large, dark, curly-haired man, with a wooden stump instead of a leg, who was playing on a set of pipes like those played by Papageno in *The Magic Flute*. This very sweet music sounded in the empty street like a shower of silver coins falling on the lava paving, but alas, none rewarded the musician. Used as we were to the harsh quality of Sicilian music, to the barrel organs, here crowned with bells and tambourines, to the braying trumpets of the fortune-tellers, to the purring drone and strident clamour of the zampognari when they come down from the hills with their huge bagpipes and long wooden trumpets to celebrate the Nativity, we were unprepared for this gentle, dulcet sound.

The streets in the busier part of the town were crowded with carts, either painted in vivid colours or unpainted but richly carved. Some of these were full of blocks of sulphur, which, as they were rattled and bumped along, left behind them a subtle suggestion of fire-and-brimstone, and a narrow trail of primrose-coloured powder on the dark lava pavement. Other carts were loaded with oranges, or piled up with lemons, whose diverse scale of golden tones finished the harmony of colouring so well, made them so complete, that they became almost too satisfying a sight, too much like some perfect model or painted toy, while, as they went by, their sharp aromatic scent conquered for the moment the more normal smells of Sicilian streets. Then another cart would appear, lumbering past us noisily, and laden with earthenware pitchers of a beautiful Greek shape, of the same design as those used here many centuries before the time of Christ.

In the poorer parts of the town the walls of the

low, box-like houses were plastered over with the placards of the marionette theatres—placards in the shrillest hues, and drawn in a manner half Byzantine, half 1840, like the Hoxton prints. There was something in their appearance that indicated them as specially designed, like the brightly-painted signs over Russian shops, for an almost wholly illiterate population. In spite of this, here were also to be found posters giving poetic accounts of the fireworks, musical and otherwise, which would celebrate this year's *festa* of St Agatha. These documents, full of the most Gongoresque and flowery descriptive passages, were issued by the Mayor and Corporation ; while also near these, and dwarfing the smaller ones of the marionette theatres, were posted up vast sheets, heralding the advent of a German circus, and depicting a young lady with golden hair, black waistcoat, pink tights and a dog-whip, pirouetting on one foot in the midst of a number of particularly black-striped and snarling tigers. The reading matter below gave one quite a new idea of the terrors of the drawing-room and social life, for the young lady and her feline friends were announced as—

"Miss Charles and her eighteen Ferocious
Debutantes"

—an announcement which made one long, like Nero, to witness an evenly-matched battle between these eighteen innocents and a team of dowagers chosen with equal care. How much more exciting would this be than the fiercest quarrel with vicar or servants, or the opening of even the most thrilling of bazaars!

In among the tortuous lanes wandered ragged children buying prickly-pears, that looked like little conventional flames, or a glass of lemonade at shrilly-painted stalls that gleamed with polished brass, or hurrying to find the fortune-teller whose trumpet could be heard in the distance. A young man, dark as a gypsy, he holds in one hand his trumpet, in the other a large glass bottle or square box, full of clear water, balanced on the end of a wooden pole. You give him money and he presses a button. A small black devil, with horns and tail, made of celluloid or a similar substance, can then be seen diving through the water, and you are presented with a printed form which foretells the happenings of your life. While we were having our fortunes told, the door of one of the houses, that, covered with placards, looked like gaudily-coloured boxes, opened, and out of it stepped, clad in brown-hooded robe and wearing sandals, a mendicant friar. This one was a hunchback, and looked as if he were a figure walking out of the decoration of an illuminated missal. He was a very queer survival of the Middle Ages, and surprised us hardly less than if we had seen a knight in armour on his way to a tourney.

Catania is famous for the manufacture of

Discursions

mandolins and guitars ; many of those that sound by lake and mountain in the Italian night are made here : so that outside every other house are hanging clusters of these unvarnished instruments, made of a pale yellow wood, and looking, with their full contours, like bunches of mellow gourds and golden melons hung out to ripen in the sun. If the music of all these instruments were to issue from this one city on a still night, it would be borne many hundreds of miles out to sea, till it must sound to the mariners like the sweet voices of the Syrens that were heard over these same waters so long ago. Even in those legendary times Catania must have been very like what it is now, in life and general appearance. And in this long continuity of the life of the people lies one of the charms of Mediterranean cities, such as Catania and Naples. Other great towns were sacked and despoiled by man, more destructive than ever were earthquake or volcano — Rome, even, is said to have lain empty for seventy years—and, with each fresh conquest, the life and appearance of those cities changed. But here a conquest makes no difference. The conqueror is assimilated almost immediately, so great is the power, so intense the character of climate and situation, the conditions imposed by sea and fiery mountain. These cities were never destroyed but they rose again immediately, being trained to it by their guardian volcanoes. And such is the wealth of the land

184

that, ever since men began to trade, there have been here great cities, fairs and festivals. St Agatha was no doubt some nymph, and the devil in the bottle was once Pan ; but fire always crowned the mountain, the streets were always full of dark gesticulating men, while the women watched quietly from their balconies.

iii

Oranges in Mamble

THE train started from Syracuse very punctually—not more than twenty minutes behind its scheduled time. "*Un orario perfetto*" the guard remarked with legitimate pride.

But then things are altering in Italy. It is only a few days since the incredibly dirty young cabman, who drove me along roads as dusty as ever they were, turned round to say—by way of starting a conversation—"You noticed, no doubt, the new suit that I was wearing for the Festival of St Andrew; a beautiful suit; I shall wear it again for Christmas." After imparting this piece of information he proceeded to give a brief account of his career. Yes, he was the son of my old friend Rafaele, the cabman—the eleventh son, but five were dead—and he was not the one who had sent his father that very sympathetic new hat from Catanzaro in Calabria. No, that son was there in a grocer's business; while himself had only recently left the Carabinieri . . . yes, a fine regiment. But the Discipline . . . ! For being half-an-hour late . . . half-an-hour, mind you . . . one was awarded ten days in prison! So that he hadn't been sorry to finish his military service. Not, though, that I was to

186

conclude that he was anti-militarist. Oh no!
When he drove a Fascist, he was Fascist; when
a Liberal, Liberal; when the Communists come
back, and he drives them, Communist! What
was he really? A cabman, like his father—who,
at the age of sixty-seven, could still drink two
bottles of good red wine. . . .

Similarly, our engine, on this occasion, appeared
to decide suddenly, after twenty minutes of hesita-
tion, that it was a steam engine, and with a piercing scream started on its way along the flat coast,
the eye - blue sea or brown lagoons on one side,
deep groves of orange and lemon on the other.

The little box-like painted houses on the island
dwindled, grew smaller and smaller, but were still
very visible under this light, fierce even in February.
There was about them a certain air of unreality,
a brightness that was too bright, a silhouette that
was unusually defined. No haze, such as the one
that hangs over Naples or Palermo, diminishing
their splendour, was visible from the distance. The
houses looked almost too square and unbroken in
their shape, for they have no chimneys; no coal
or wood is burned except by the steamers that lurk
close to the Fountain of Arethusa. Charcoal is the
only fuel of the town, and the air is quivering in
its natural brightness. The hills showed in the
distance, and far away, hanging over the horizon,
Etna displayed its perfection of form, covered with
snow that seemed to take every colour in the sky

Discursions

above and earth beneath, to float, light as a soap-
bubble, just over the world. The brown fields that
lay on our right were broken with masses of blue
iris; the spiky buds of the asphodel were about to
burst their sheaths; the detail of these meadows
was very noticeable, each plant, as yet severe in
form, precise in line as the flower-plates in early
nineteenth-century books of botany, seemed to be
drawn in the shrillest green against this quiet
background. There followed low clouds of cherry
and almond, anchored not much above the ground,
moving a little with each slight breeze, very
fragile and easily shattered, alternating with dark
mysterious groves of orange and lemon, carefully
hung with their various red-gold and green-gold
lamps. These trees struck a distinctly early
Renaissance note in contrast to the blossoming
fruit-trees, which were either Oriental in inspiration or rococo as a Dresden figure; while the
ascetic flower-forms in the fields seemed either
Greek or early nineteenth-century. And of all
these mixed styles, the orange and lemon trees are
the most perfect, the most beautiful. Under the
shadow of their glossy, green leaves grew tall,
slender flowers with yellow bells. Their shelter was
gloomy, yet calm and peaceful—a fitting resting-
place for some figure come to life out of the
early masters, some Madonna weary with the
constant pose, and with the passing centuries.
The trees, too, are serene as the picture from

which the figure has escaped, classical yet luxuriant
in form, hung with ivory blossoms and gold lamps.

As the train bumped along I could not help
wondering why orange-trees are at present in such
disfavour in the best circles. For they are—of
that there can be no doubt! I am not, though,
so ashamed as I ought to be of my liking for
orange-trees, fruit or flower; for a writer in one
of the weekly papers, a poet and bird-fancier, has
made public the confession that from two books of
travel sent him for review, one volume on Labrador,
the other on Italy and Spain, he chose the former,
because such books as the latter, he avers, are
filled with purple patches describing the orange
and lemon groves of the South. An optimist is
our bird-fancier, since one can travel through half
Spain and three quarters of Italy without catching
a glimpse of even a captive orange in a shop window. Personally I admit to liking both oranges
and an occasional purple patch, but putting my
own preferences aside, if one is lucky enough to
find these peculiarly beautiful trees decorating
the landscape, what can one do but gratefully
acknowledge the fact? English hedgerows, and
the warblers that frequent them, are left behind;
and why should one repine? It is no use com-
plaining, like that other bird-fancying bard who,
visiting Florence last autumn, admitted that he
liked the town but missed the golden aureole, and
subsequently deplored the extinction of the Ptero-

Discursions

Dactyl as a verse measure. Nor need the presence of an orange-tree, or even a whole grove of them, suggest any softness of scenery; for they can be found contrasting with the most rugged and fantastically savage landscapes. And why should an orange be less mentionable, in prose or verse, than a ploughed field or an ale-house? It is no use for a writer to be self-conscious.

"I have never been to Mamble," sings another very eminent English poet, perhaps rather vaguely:

> "I've never been to Mamble
> That lies above the Theme,
> So I wonder who's in Mamble
> And whether people seem
>
> Who brew and breed along there
> As lazy as the name,
> And whether any song there
> Sets ale-house wits aflame."

Without any pretension to pronounce authoritatively on the subject, I should judge the answer to the latter question to be in the negative. Surely oranges are preferable to this Mamble-pamble business? And I suggest to our bird-fancier that Marvell's lines:

> "He hangs in shades the orange bright,
> Like golden lamps in a green night,"

in spite of their content, are superior as poetry to those other ones quoted above. Enough has been heard of the Mermaid Tavern: yet the fact that

Oranges in Mamble

those who met there met in an ale-house, no more
makes them into ale-house wits than the fact that
certain ale-house wits meet now in a public-house
converts it into a Mermaid tavern. But perhaps,
after all, the ale-house wits *have* become a little
inflamed . . .? From this distance I cannot hope
to secure a copy of *The London Mercury* by which
to judge. . . .

As regards intrinsic beauty, there is nothing
necessarily wrong about it, one presumes? Because an orange - tree is, indubitably, a beautiful
object—is it, then, debarred from being the subject
for either painting or poetry? But there, again,
is our trouble. Ale-house wits, however aflame,
are apt to be a trifle slow. For years they went
out after pure beauty, chasing it and worrying it
until it became necessary to point out to them that
however beautiful was a rose as a natural object,
a poem about one was not necessarily a beautiful
poem. After some years they grasped this, but
completely mistook its import, jumping to the
conclusion that if a poem about a rose was not
necessarily a beautiful poem, then a poem about
a football field or a slaughter - house must be a
beautiful poem. Ever since we have been deluged
with strong, stark, facing-facts poems, which, alas,
are obviously by the same authors as the previous
rather precious ones. "Oranges are out this
year, sir, and Labrador's in!"

An orange-grove, then, is perhaps a little tame

Discursions

in the quality of its beauty—not to those who
have seen one, for there abides, in the darkness
under and about the trees, a great mystery—but to
those who have preconceived ideas of it. Yet it
is surely, even thus, no more tame than the best
English landscapes, the chief merit of which is
usually their atmosphere of " niceness," comfort,
and well - being ; for the scenery of our country,
when it becomes savage, goes red, is intolerable.
One patch of heather outvies in depression all the
frozen waves that rattle and scratch at the iron
coast of Labrador, would put to immediate rout
the wildest buffalo, the fiercest bison, and when
in blossom, has a tone of colour so infinitely re-
pulsive, so glaring yet muddy withal, that to find
its equal, all the picture-postcards of sunset-Egypt
may be searched in vain. Yet being a bird-
fancier myself, after my own fashion, I can forgive
the heather much of its colour for the shelter it
affords young grouse.

If a writer is surrounded by either heather or
oranges, it is, in any case, up to him to make
the best of it. Faith can only remove mountains.
The heather, the oranges, would be growing in
the plain disclosed by their removal. From my
window I can discern, very far across the wide
bay, the broken temples of Pæstum. With the
best will in the world I cannot bring myself to
like Greek temples—at any rate in their present
condition. I cannot speak of the time when they

were gaudy with light blues, terra-cottas and vivid yellows. At present they have little intrinsic beauty, only that accidental one, "romantic," and literary. But the fact that I do not like them does not prevent their being there, does it? Thus, too, the bird-fancier must endure the irritation caused by reading of orange and lemon groves, letting his mind be solaced by the shooting flames of ale-house wit, by memories of Mamble and its muddy dykes. Like the author of the poem about that place, I have never been to Mamble, so, unlike him, I shall not write about it. But I have seen orange-groves, have eaten oranges, and have enjoyed doing both; and shall, therefore, write about them without fear or prejudice. One has to use the material that is to hand—though not everyone agrees with this sentiment.

"I have been acquainted with the work of the *best* poets from my youth up," wrote an angry old lady to the editor of a paper that had published one of my sister's poems, "Byron, Matthew Arnold, Tennyson, Wordsworth—though somehow Keats did not find his way on to our shelves until later—but of what do Miss Sitwell's poems consist but words, words, words?" But since a poet is no hewer of wood nor in all cases, apparently, a drawer of water, of what other material but words can a poem be made? Even the late Alfred Lord Tennyson did not altogether despise them. And, after all, the angry old lady's letter would not amount to much without words, though it is possible that the rhythm would remain. There is something splendid about the swing of those lines:

"But of what do Miss Sitwell's poems consist
But words, words, words?"

Mr Kipling, too, I think, must have crept later on to that shelf . . . in the strange company of Keats.

Let us, therefore, sing the praise of orange-grove, orange-tree and the fruit it bears. Where it grows you will find the best climate, the most beautiful of European buildings. There is Monreale, with the exception of Santa Sophia at Constantinople, and San Vitale at Ravenna, the most beautiful of Byzantine churches—which is to say the most beautiful of all churches. There is Cefalu; there is the Cappella Palatina at Palermo with its honeycomb ceiling. The interiors of these churches are a golden haze, through which can be distinguished the lank, lonely figures of saints, hermits and holy men. With their deep, piercing eyes they gaze at you from the golden walls, vast figures rising out of the haze with the strange dignity of another world. Here is an art that has never been improved upon, if it has ever been equalled. The iron tooth of the restorer has gnawed at them in vain, unable to rob these sanctuaries of their grandeur. Even the coloured portrait of King Victor Emmanuel III., stencilled up on the serpentine slab in the centre of the wall facing the altar, has been unable to deprive the Cappella Palatina of its glory.

For the English these churches have a special interest, since they were built by kings of Norman blood. The orange-groves are nowhere out of sight from these ancient buildings, and form a fit setting for them. From Monreale, high up on its hill, the groves sweep down to the golden shell of the sea, forming one of the most magnificent views in the world. The whole valley beneath is full of these varying golden and green flames, which lick the very walls of the city. Then come the golden buildings of the town itself, and away, beyond, on a fine day can be distinguished two lines of cones, faint blue and distant as the background of some early Italian picture, floating above the horizon, like sentinels, or like pyramids erected to mark the way of some vast ceremonial procession — but these volcanoes can be seen only on the finest days. Everywhere the very stylised beauty of the orange-tree fits in with that of the works-of-art. Then, for those who admire Greek Art, there is Pæstum, with its orange-groves and malarious swamps. There are the temples at Girgenti, the theatres and tombs of Syracuse, and in Southern Italy a whole world of broken-down art, which to enumerate would take up a long lifetime and fill a thousand folios.

The orange-tree itself is a pleasant object, made from a pleasant and sweet wood, with clusters of golden globes that illumine the most radiant day ; and, to set them, it is given the darkest and glossiest of green leaves ; the ivory flowers, which seem tied in little knots upon the branches, have a fragance stronger than that of any other flower ; and the golden globes themselves are cool and refreshing as nectar. About the whole tree there is a design, a balance, a geometrical intention and sense of grouping, an economy and right use of colour, that make it rank almost as high as a work - of - art. An orange - tree, indeed, reflects more credit than does man upon its Maker.

The fruit itself is as admirably designed as the tree that bears it ; it has a golden skin to keep it clean, and is divided-up in a way that marks it out as a fruit intended for the use and pleasure of human beings. It is useful as well as delicious.

Like tea and coffee, the orange was first intro-duced into England for medicinal purposes, and even now is stated to contain " vitamines," those potent but mysterious attributes. It may, there-fore, be presumed that its juice has health-giving qualities. Nor has it ever shared the fate of the apple, and been identified with evil. How any man or woman, brought up on Genesis, can ever bear to see, let alone taste, a Russet or a Cox's Orange Pippin without shame, has always puzzled me ! But no such disgrace clings to the fair name of orange.

In England the orange-tree calls up the idea of

Oranges in Mamble

an orangery, of Hampton Court and Kensington
Palace, and the works of the two greatest English
architects, Inigo Jones and Wren. Over the
minds of children its fruit exercises an extraordinary fascination ; even the geography lesson
is for the moment made more tolerable by the
sweet ingenious comparison of the earth to an
orange turning on its axis, while King William III.
remains one of the most popular of nursery monarchs, being invested with an eternal charm, a
fragrance that percolates through his name, completely obliterating in the child-mind that "fatal
charm" of his predecessors, or the romantic claims
of the two Pretenders. William of Orange, a
beautiful name!

The peel of the fruit makes a very cunning trap
for the feet of old men, and to fall on it would
be suitable punishment for the blasphemies of the
bird-fancier.

In reality it may be surmised, perhaps, that what
the latter objects to in Southern Italy, Spain, and
Sicily is not so much the prevalence of orange
or lemon as the existence of innumerable works-
of-art ; for the multitude of these, and not of the
groves at which he shudders, is the essential difference between these countries and Labrador.
Afraid to admit it, he has "blamed it" (as Mr
Kipling would say) on the orange. The anti-
æsthetic stunt has already been woefully over-
done, and is now more boring than any purple patch

Discursions

could ever become. Anyone who believes in it should be made to undergo a Tour of Empire. Samuel Butler first let it loose on us, and it came at a good moment; but even the most fervent of Butler's admirers must admit that, though what he did not know about priests and parents was not worth knowing, his reactions toward works-of-art, his æsthetic perceptions, are by no means interesting or remarkable. Anyone who, out of affection for Butler's writings, has made a pious pilgrimage to Varallo, will in future avoid those things that he praises. His dislikes were well founded and stimulating; his likings, especially æsthetic ones, are not to be trusted. Indeed, Varallo, in its way, stands for all that Butler by his other writings condemned, for was there ever, in the whole world of artifice, such a Sunday Afternoon in South Kensington?

It may be concluded then that, if our reviewer dislikes works-of-art, he will abominate especially those that are either particularly artificial or, on the other hand, devoid of literary associations. For in spite of his dislike and fear of purple patches, he is probably unable to resist those lines about the Gioconda being older than the rocks among which she sits; but no one has yet attempted to write in that way (they will later, however) about a crumpled-napkin-and-apple picture (christened a *Crumpler*, by Mr Walter Sickert), even if it is as bare, stark, and bony as the sea-coast of

Oranges in Mamble

Labrador. The *Mona Lisa* is a purple patch in painting, but a still-life by Cézanne — though a great work-of-art—is bony and plain and has no smile in it; yet little incense will be swung to it by our bird-fancier. That is the worst of these art-simpletons; when they get real simplicity, they do not care for it. Another bird-loving writer looked at a drawing by Matisse—a drawing as simple—albeit artful—as a drawing can be, and then roared at me, as if I were responsible for it, " My child of *five* can do that sort of thing "; but when asked from which side of the family the boy inherited his talent, was silent. If modern art, though, enrages them, so does that of the eighteenth century. By a simple process of un-reason, the orange calls up that age to them—Orange—Orangery—William of Orange—Queen Mary—Queen Anne—Palaces—Ballrooms—Allegorical Frescoes—Alexander Pope. How artificial! How different to the sublime innocence, the un-studied simplicity of

> " I've never been to Mamble
> That lies above the Theme,
> So I wonder who's in Mamble
> And whether people seem . . ."

And the only oranges that are tolerable to them are those that lie, exposed for sale in their wooden boxes, in the window of the village post-office at Mamble.

iv

Noto

NOTO, to which we journeyed from Syracuse, would please the lover of Labrador even less than the orange-groves by which it is surrounded. Here is no haphazard and random collection of buildings, but the ideal, the model town of its time, for no city has ever been planned more as a work-of-art. Placed on a hill some way distant from and above the sea, approached through gently rising fields that in this early spring appear at first to be snow-covered, their smooth, soft planes still preserving in some mysterious way the iridescent hues of sunrise, so thick are the drifts of cherry and almond blossom, or by roads hedged with prickly-pears that stretch out their twisted arms and stiff joints, is the great collection of golden domes, spires, turrets, towers and wide platforms that compose this remarkable city. A large one it seems, as we walk through the sweet-smelling country that has a scent of fruit blossom and herbs, thyme, bay, myrtle, and many unknown sharp, aromatic perfumes. In reality it shelters only twenty thousand people, but the buildings are so imposing, there are so many churches, palaces, monasteries, triumphal arches and public edifices, that it appears much larger, much more important. Whole quarries of golden stone have been emptied endlessly on the hill-side.

The older city that occupied the site was destroyed by the earthquake of 1693. But the people of Noto, quite undismayed, set themselves to the task of rebuilding, and were here not content with the improvising of makeshifts or stage-backgrounds, such as sprang up in Acireale after the same event. No sign is here of degradation or debasement; no brutal masks or leering ogres grin at you from the wall and balcony. Here, at least, full advantage is taken of the opportunity offered, and the builders built for all eternity.

The reason for this difference of architectural outlook, between towns so near together and similarly afflicted, may be that the citizens of Noto, which had been destroyed only once in this way during all its history, were therefore able to regard the earthquake as an unfortunate incident, while those of Acireale, at the full mercy of both earthquake and lava stream, had now to regard the recurring destruction of their homes as one of the few certainties of existence.

Nor are the buildings at Noto at all like those others of the same date — and perhaps more beautiful if less complete—at Syracuse, only twenty miles away. For the piazza at Syracuse has three superb monuments of this very epoch, two palaces and the rococo façade of the cathedral. The latter

Discursions

is an object of supreme interest, skill, and loveliness, for it masks the old Greek temple, which is still the chief place of worship in the city ; and masks it so worthily that no lover of architecture, however fond of Greek Art, would wish it away. Looking down the street at the side, one can see the twenty - five - century - old columns of the Greek temple, which, with the intervals between them built-up, form the outside walls of the modern church, and above, the Greek entablature! How typical of the warring yet mingling cultures of Syracuse, where, in every street, buildings of every age, nearly all of them beautiful of their kind, can be found knotted together. Inside the old temple the two central rows of columns are standing, are yet supporting the roof, while the chapels running down each side of the church must be very much the same in appearance as when the Greek tongue was the language spoken in the street. The façade, delicate but simple, is built of a golden stone, much the same as that used at Noto ; while certain decorations are carried out in another stone of a paler yellow. It is planned for those strong effects of light and shadow only to be obtained in southern climates, where recesses have a mystery and solemnity, their surroundings a gaiety, lacking in Northern Europe. This church front is both a little more subtle and a little less pompous than its contemporaries at Noto. But then at Syracuse it is necessary to consider the other buildings in the

SYRACUSE : THE CATHEDRAL

Noto

piazza, in the town, while the Noto of the same period was non-existent, or lay buried. For perhaps twenty years there was on this hill-side a whole forest of scaffolding. So long had the poles been planted in fertile Sicilian ground, that many of them were like maypoles, having little wreaths of tender green shoots clinging to their tops. And swaying high among these tree-tops were the floating cradles and trestles, from which fell bird-like cries and wailing fragments of song, as the workmen in their white clothes cried out to one another across the silent paths of the forest. There were great sounds of hammering up in the air, and the figures moved easily among the branches, their white clothes flapping out against the blue sky. And beneath their hands, and hidden by the sprouting forest, other more permanent leaves and flowers were unfolded and blossoming—leaves and flowers of golden stone and of a thousand intricate designs. No traffic moved along these dark paths in the forest for twenty years, until one morning all the swaying trees were cut, and as if by magic the golden city was found beneath them in full blossom.

By the end of the second decade of the eighteenth century that forest must have been felled, and this extraordinary town revealed in its entirety, the work, no doubt, as to general planning and design, of one man—probably a monk. But this fact is difficult to substantiate, since the citizens of Noto are ignorant of the creators of the treasure among which they move as were the citizens of Benin. Yet, in spite of the date of this town, its character belongs as much to the seventeenth as to the eighteenth century. In inspiration the buildings are grandiose and sombre, infused with the spirit of the earlier epoch, while the detail of them is gay and delicate, full of the spirit of the latter age. The whole scale, the planning of the place, is magnificent, intended to impress ; yet the architect has not been content to create a vast and heartless machine, but has been able to give full vent to a lively, original, and rather laughing genius. Certainly for this flight he was mounted on a Pegasus, and the winged children of that steed can yet be observed tethered above our heads, under the very window of the palaces, supporting the flying balconies with their outspread wings, their forefeet curved, ready to leap up over the roofs beyond. For Noto, above all other towns, even before Syracuse, is sacred to the arts and rites of the balcony. Every house in Noto is a palace, in fact as well as in name, and a splendid balcony bellies out under every palace window, supported by these horses, by eagles about to swoop on their prey, by Chinamen with slanting eyes and flat noses, by fierce Turks in vast turbans and a thousand other devices. None of these figures are horrible or realistic as are those at Acireale, but pleasant if rather legendary. The railings of the balconies are very beautiful, with a full sweep and curve, while

Noto

at the two corners are invariably hung huge blossoms of wrought iron, rose, carnation, or sunflower, measuring a foot or two across.

Noto appears to have developed an architecture peculiar to itself, related to, though easily distinguishable from, that of other Sicilian or Italian towns. In this respect it cannot be said to equal Lecce, which boasted a whole school of architects and architecture, an indigenous style, yet one which would be a credit to any city. At Noto, however, we have but a beautiful variation on a familiar theme; while at Lecce both theme and variations are original. But after Lecce, which must come to the stranger as a surprising revelation of beauty, nothing had been so pleasantly unexpected as this town on the hill. An extraordinarily fine example of town-planning, the width of street, the avenues of trees, the playing-off of one church against another, one palace against another, the broad golden platforms and shallow stairways, the architectural screens, the magnificence of the public buildings (of which the colonnaded market-place is a typical example), the sense of co-ordination, the utter lack of muddle, make it look at first sight almost too good to be true. It seems a complete realisation of one of those large folding plates which are found in the architectural books of the late seventeenth and early eighteenth centuries—such as that one by Fischer von Erlach—the model town of its

Discursions

age. The grandeur and size of it are like the
plate ; so, too, are the avenues of clipped and
flat-topped trees that lie in the street. Looking
at one of these engravings, we had imagined
that nowhere had it been possible to realise this
ideal, since no town could or would divest itself
willingly of its entire past. It must have been
impossible, we had thought, either to pull down or
to rebuild on this scale. No town could, surely,
in that age ever have afforded to rid itself of en-
cumbrances and still have left-over the necessary
wealth with which to create. But here circumstances, combined with the riches of Church and
nobles, conspired to make the miracle possible.
The outward and visible history of the town was
destroyed in one night and at no cost ; but the
wealth remaining was sufficient for the need, the
pride of the citizen adequate to the occasion. Nor
is the effect so frigid as might be expected after
a consideration of such plates, for the stone is so
warm in colour, the details so spirited, the life so
vivid, the shelter of the dark green trees so blue
and restful, that there is no air of the machine
triumphing over man.

The city consists of six or seven terraces or wide
platforms, one above the other, on the hill-side, looking toward the sea. Each of these terraces forms a
street of remarkable breadth—the main one as wide
as the Hyde Park end of Piccadilly ; in many places,
indeed, wider, for the churches are set back a long

way, and approached by colossal flights of shallow steps broken by several landings. Some of these sweep down to the street in one straight line, others divide into cunning, curving, double staircases. It can be imagined that a long, regular street with seven or eight of these ascents, alternating with high golden palaces and monasteries, is very effective—if rather tiring for the regular churchgoer. The buildings are all of the same stone; many streets being planted with these clipped trees. The churches are all alike, yet in detail different; domes alternate with towers; the façade, whether flat, receding, or projecting, has Corinthian columns crowned with ornate capitals; while over doors and windows are cut fantastic rococo scrolls and shields. Each building is well planned, with as much space as it needs, and no air of being cramped, the superficial decorations well-balanced and cleanly cut. The streets of palaces, which are narrower, intersect these broad platforms at right angles, leading up and down from one to the other, so that after walking along, beneath the shadow of tall convents, past the open sunlit spaces of the stairways, a narrowing vista is suddenly disclosed of endless balconies, a riot of leaping figures and movement, till the golden stone of the street seems, toward the horizon, to be dissolving into spray or dashing up into the air like the bright foam of a rocket.

In the main street, and in the narrower ones as

well, there are no small houses, for where ordinarily a town would degenerate into collections of low-storeyed houses and shops, here the architect has erected the most elaborate of screens. The shops on the ground floor, the living-rooms above, are set in a façade worthy of any palace, and above, through the empty, magnificent windows of the upper storeys, decorated with scrolls, with wreaths of flowers and swags of fruit, shows the deep per-spective of blue sky and snow-white cloud. Down in the street the avenues of old trees give shelter to pavements that in the summer would otherwise be too full of heat and sunlight, and their flattened and smooth green tops offer very pleasant paths for the wind from the sea to run along. Indeed, from above, these paths look so soft, yet so solid, that we are half tempted to run along them ourselves! The churches, monasteries, and palaces have a fine dramatic air, though it must be admitted that all this civic and ecclesiastical magnificence frames in a rather sordid, if vivid, life. The people of the town have their own homes, such as they are; but for the visitor there is no hotel, nor any place where he can eat or rest with comfort. But then a stranger is not to be encouraged except as a brief diversion for idle crowds. These stand about beneath the trees, in the broad spaces, clad in cloaks against the spring winds, or with shawls and rugs encircling their shoulders. It is an affair of deep voices and gruff laughter, for the women are kept securely in their houses in an Oriental seclusion. The wine-shops are full of smoke and sound.

As in so many out-of-the-way districts, good building seems to have continued here right down into the middle of the last century. The triumphal arch through which the city is reached belongs to the Empire period, while the theatre, a handsome one, was built as late as 1840; these harmonise well with the rest of the architecture, and unlike most towns, the convenience of the other monuments must have been considered. For architecture, like many other things, depends to a certain extent on good manners; to put a vulgar, ugly, or glaring edifice, in a totally different style from its surroundings, next to an old church or palace, is, architecturally, the worst of bad manners. It is a slight, an insult almost, of which no person of feeling would wish to be guilty.

It is noticeable that the courtyards and interior decorations of the palaces are uninteresting. Even the wealth of Noto was, presumably, not boundless, and must have already been expended on the outside of the house long before the inside was touched. The wonder is, not that the interiors are so dull, but that the façades are so beautiful. The churches, on the other hand, have quite adequate interiors; though these, even, possess little of unusual interest except for altars, carried out in coloured lacquer, which are reminiscent of

Discursions

those in churches at Toledo, though neither so
fantastic in conception nor so unexpected in
colour.

Another speciality of the town is the number
of heraldic shields which decorate it so plentifully,
very charming and graceful in line. It is unusual
to find good heraldry of so late a period.

The upper platforms of the town contain more
palaces than churches; indeed the number of noble
families who appear to live in Noto is prodigious:
the possession of a coat-of-arms, a hundred quarterings, and a soft-sounding title seems to be the
inherited lot of two out of every three of its
citizens. The crowd in the market-place, we
should judge, would in no way compare with the
mob at a fashionable reception, the chatter of the
wine-shops could never hope to rival the din in
the large rooms of one of these palaces, when full
of the local nobility. Be that as it may, the
Barone di San Giacomo was, undoubtedly, giving
a party that afternoon—a party that had started
at eleven A.M. with the arrival of the train from
Syracuse, and is rumoured to have lasted until
midnight. For, not content with the nobles
and dignitaries of his native town, the enterpris-
ing Baron had called in the neighbouring horde
from Syracuse. And in the train with us had
been armies of flashing-eyed young ladies and
spotlessly-dressed men.

The façade of the palace was a fine one, and

Noto

from the wide - open windows a very animated
chattering and drone, such as can be heard only
in the most Southern European countries, poured
out on to the projecting balconies, and from them
dripped down steadily on to the street below.
And in that street were two private carriages, for
so remote a district a sign of position and wealth,
a symbol of luxury, and, to a connoisseur, more
interesting even than the discovery of that
" Berlino" at Lecce which we have detailed elsewhere. The polished panels of the doors were
decorated with heraldic shields and coats-of-arms
of impressive size, taking up nearly a square foot
of varnished surface. Heraldry was, obviously, a
living thing here. Nor were these shields mov-
able or removable, as are so many of those smaller
ones on the carriages in Naples, where several
noble families often share, for economic reasons,
the same carriage, but are able, when they drive
out in state, to fix on to the doors, by some ingenious piece of mechanism, their own appropriate
coat-of-arms. For the Neapolitan nobles are proud
as the Spanish, and no stranger, and even less a
friend, must be allowed to discover the dire extent
of their poverty ; while, above all, it must never
be suspected that cruel circumstances have forced
such illustrious families to share the same vehicle.
But these shields were, quite definitely, immovable,
painted on the door! In fact, the carriages were
entitled to be considered as "genuine collectors'

pieces." Each one was shaped like a brougham, but larger, more curved in front, while on each box sat a tiger, with folded arms, and top-hat, beside the liveried coachman!

Somehow the carriages and their attendants, the golden streets and green trees, seemed familiar. I was acquainted, surely, with some scene akin to it, and then the outlines of this picture began to harden in the mind. Just as the whole town realised the apparently unattainable perfection of a plate in one of those old architectural books, so this was the realisation of another imaginary but idealised scene—one of those scenes blazoned within the lid of a cigar-box!

Oh, those lovely worlds of the imagination, blended of past and future! Why does no benefactor collect these only examples of true commercial art, and present them to the nation? Why is there no amateur of cigar-boxes, as of cigarette cards or postage stamps? They, alone, of all things, have inherited the improbable and impalpable beauty of illuminated missals. Their palaces of gold dust expose to the gold glare of the tropic sun various cool but glittering surfaces of rock crystal (for out of no such ordinary material as glass can these windows have been fashioned), under a violet sky, flecked with little sunset clouds made likewise of gold dust. Huge golden medals, like so many balloons, hang suspended in the bright air —medals that are as large as the palaces beneath

them.   Beyond, feathery palm-trees, with stout
trunks that broaden toward the base, having both
the shape and colour of elephants' feet, salaam
before the softest of Spanish halcyons.   For one
of these fabulous birds, accompanying Columbus
on his first voyage, nested in the vicinity, and
often visits the scene, perching first on this, then
on that palm.   Then there are other palm-trees,
with greener, broader, glossy leaves, and on the
far side of the street bloom bushes of incredible
roses—red roses, pink roses with broad open faces.
Through the spaces between them show lagoons
where dusky natives, their dark faces half hidden
under mushroom-like hats, their forms fantastically clothed in striped and chequered cottons,
can be seen plucking or rolling the tobacco leaves.
In front of the palaces, among flowers that rival
them in their splendour, are ladies of a mid-
Victorian yet foreign elegance, reclining in open
barouches, drawn along by horses that paw, while
yet they hardly touch, the roads that seem paved
with gold.   On the box is a liveried footman with
cockaded top-hat and a coachman dressed in the
same style.   The footman is alert, ever in readi-
ness for the slightest murmur from his mistress;
she wishes the horses to be drawn up while she
speaks to that very dashing-looking military gentleman in a top-hat and long red coat, which contrasts
with the blue frock-coats of the other men walking
in the street.   He has side-whiskers and dark, very

Discursions

dark eyes. In her ear he whispers for a moment and then prances on again, rising up and down on his caracoling Velasquez steed; and over all in the box—though not over Noto—floats the subtle aromatic perfume of Havana.

Part iii

Fiume and d'Annunzio

i

Fiume and d'Annunzio

IT was on the shores of the Neapolitan Bay that the idea of visiting Fiume laid hold on us. Though this was nearly the last month in the year, the Sun strummed over flat roofs and feathery palm-trees, furrowed hills and undulating blue waters with an unequalled brilliancy and sparkle, as if he were some great executant displaying his virtuosity in private and for his own pleasure. And under the influence of this parade all troubles became, for the moment, minimised. To journey for a night or two to Venice and then on to d'Annunzio's small principality seemed a small matter—the icy fingers that already held Northern Italy in their grip were altogether unimaginable, while such things as passports became unimportant, mere whims of bureaucracy.

One misses so many opportunities—from caution, foresight, or the desire for a peaceful life—leaving history to be described by unintelligent individuals who have developed the faculty of witnessing events which, at the time, they misunderstand, and subsequently misrepresent. There are, of course, rare exceptions, like the younger Pliny or Marco Polo, who enable one to see the things they describe more clearly than if one had been a spectator of them; but, as a rule, the very excuse advanced on their own behalf by "Onlooker" or "Eye-witness" for being present at some catastrophe or in some adventure is, in reality, the accusation against them. They happened, they say, to be on the spot when such or such a thing transpired. In fact, like Casabianca on the burning deck, they remained while their companions, more intelligent and capable, if less dutiful, sought safety, or a more normal existence, elsewhere. And though the episode of Fiume offered little danger to the foreigner, it was a unique adventure that deserved a more sympathetic study than it would obtain from an English clergyman stranded there at the time of the poet's escapade, or from some American maiden-lady who had lost her passport and was unable to get away. For here was a small State seized and ruled by a poet; and though to many steady nineteenth-century minds his exploit seemed but a symptom of the paralysis that was creeping over Europe as a result of our all attempting, by rather violent means, to make the world Safe for Democracy, his small dominion might yet develop —if not crushed in a few weeks—into an ideal land, where the arts would flourish once more on Italian soil, where they have so often flowered before. It might even, if it survived, offer an escape from the

Fiume and d'Annunzio

Scylla and Charybdis of modern life, Bolshevism or American Capitalism—morbid states of the soul that offer to the artist the alternatives, so well summed up in a rag-time song as

> "You've got to get under!
> Get out or get under."

And, indeed, in its children (for Fascism is the child of Fiume) it has provided us with a third choice.

Certainly d'Annunzio's adventure was one unequalled in the last hundred years, because the Anglo-Saxon fear of genius—and a very well-founded fear it is—dominated Europe in the nineteenth century. No man of genius had dared to attempt to rule a Municipality, far less a State, since the rising middle-classes made such an example of Napoleon I. Napoleon III. tried it; and to a degree succeeded, but then our rulers were sure that he was no cleverer than they were, and they had known him for many years in England; since then, too, he had undergone a long period of more or less solitary confinement in a fortress, which could hardly have improved his mental powers. Except for the "mad" King of Bavaria, the Continent has had no monarch or President since 1815 who took—or even pretended to take—the faintest interest in any form of art, except exhibitions of water-colours by highly-connected but rather incompetent young ladies. Music, literature, and painting have had to become independent of patronage, a fact which is even more damaging to the possible patron than it is financially disagreeable to the exponents of these arts. Yet an intelligent, art-loving monarch would have made Europe a much more agreeable place; and art is a safer, more permanent memorial than political intrigue, court ceremonies, or an inspection of voluntary but militant charwomen. Wagner, for example, was and is a finer memorial to Ludwig II. than was the Entente to King Edward and President Loubet, or the Kiel Canal to the Emperor William.

If, in our country, music by long custom—for the English Court as late as the eighteenth century was a musical one—has in some academic form still to be referred to or acclaimed by a member of the Reigning House, it is then hailed, not for itself, but as a "Bond of Empire"; though why music more than dumb-bells or caviare, beavers or Beatie-and-Babs, should constitute a "Bond of Empire" remains rather unintelligible. After his speech, the Personage retires, to be regaled on indifferent rag - time, heralded and concluded by *God Save the King.* Poetry, too, is for ever officially identified with the *Absent-minded Beggar* and *The Hell-Gate of Soissons*, while pictures, one imagines, are equally links in the Thin Red Line —but battle pictures and portraits, presumably, more than landscapes by Cézanne or those funny old things by Giotto. And yet . . . "Giotto as a Bond of Empire" . . . makes a good caption.

Fiume and d'Annunzio

On the other hand, members of the Royal Houses still have to refer to the Arts, even if rather misguidedly, while Presidents of Republics need not even do lip-service to this side of life.

But d'Annunzio was a great poet, devoted passionately to music as well as literature—music was, in the Constitution of Fiume,[1] declared the national religion—and for a time his realm appeared to offer an escape from the normal European misery and vulgarity. But we ought to have known then that no Power "would tolerate for an instant" the vicinity of a ruling poet. Whatever the artistic possibilities of his venture, they were killed; though the political, subversive ones were driven back to their own country, to survive in a more aggravated form, to conquer, and to be a direct challenge everywhere to the Established Order that had been responsible for their defeat. For though many of our journals at present belaud Fascism (to which they were formerly violently opposed), thinking it now a splendid, vulgar, noisy, money-grubbing, castor-oil-administering weapon of Law-and-Order, they are mistaken; and the more they know this movement, the less will they like it! They have been taken in once more by the showy, disagreeable side of things; for the hymn of the Fascisti is merely a libel on the thousands of eager, energetic, clever men who compose that body. And the Fascisti, for their part, remember the

[1] See Appendix.

221

outrageous attacks on d'Annunzio which preceded the present fawning on Mussolini.

One of the most curious features of the onslaughts on the poet by the majority of the English and American Press was that he was arraigned for those very faults which—if they existed in him at all—he shared in a very minor degree with those who attacked him. He was accused of an Imperialistic outlook, a love of money, a love of power, and a love of sensationalism! But if these suggestions contained a grain of truth, he should have been the idol of the Yellow Press the world over. . . . The real accusation against him—that he was an artist, and therefore unpopular with the leaders of a commercial Europe—was never mentioned. The truth only peeped out through such a heading as "Fresh Outburst by Crazy Poet." For, like Lenin and Trotsky, d'Annunzio has been, time and time again, assigned to the asylum, or triumphantly assassinated, in the columns of the English newspapers.

The English, in spite of poetry being essentially their art, have, perhaps, never particularly cared for poets as individuals [1]; and a poet of d'Annunzio's

---

[1] In case I am accused of exaggerating that dislike for the poet which is generally felt if anything unusual about him suggests that such is his profession, I may perhaps be allowed to relate a story of the schooldays of one famous poet :

A few months ago I sat next, at luncheon, to an impressive old gentleman, who owned to eighty-six years. A fine old machine he looked, as he told me how much he had enjoyed his life, and how

Fiume and d'Annunzio

type is peculiarly antipathetic to them. For though the Italian is a far greater writer than was Byron, there are certain obvious resemblances between them: Byron's personality, in his own time, wielded as powerful an influence as d'Annunzio's; both have left their mark for ever on Continental literature; both provided gossip and scandal for the boudoirs; both sought refuge in political adventure; both may be said to have betrayed the British public—for the latter always states that it likes poetry-with-a-message-in-it, regarding the poet, apparently, as a messenger-boy between Heaven and the Suburbs —yet, if it really likes this form of the art (with a message dropped in it like sugar in a nice cup of tea), nothing can exceed its fury if the message is one which it does not care for or expect! So that, in the end, we ascertain that what it actually demands is poetry with a message which it likes, or to which at any rate it has grown accustomed. Thus d'Annunzio, like Swinburne and Byron, was

little sympathy he felt for those who did not appreciate their conditions or get on well with their fellow-men. "If a man—or a schoolboy for that—does not get on well," he remarked, "it's his own fault. I well remember when I first went to Eton, the head-boy called us al together and, pointing to a little fellow with a mass of curly red hair, said: 'If ever you see that boy, kick him—and if you are too far off to kick him, throw a stone at him!' He was a fellow named Swinburne," he added—"used to write poetry for a time, I believe, but I don't know what became of him." Biographers, please note! For this is the sort of story about the poets which we all suspect but are never told. For the biographers, usually respectable literary men, are far too busy making the poet's peace with the public, and praising the virtue of his private life, to tell us of these little details.

Discursions

first accused of bearing no message; and then reviled for the message he brought.

Indeed, if d'Annunzio resembles Byron in force of character and in his political escapades, as a poet, in his worship of form and love of words, he is nearer to Swinburne. And truly it is his poetry and writings that are of interest; not his politics. His written words are still there for us to read, their meaning moving swiftly, rather dimly, through the glorious phrases, as a salamander, half obscured by the smoke of a great fire, might move through the flame. For fire is d'Annunzio's element, as, legendarily, it is the salamander's. In no other medium but flame could these two live.

It has already been suggested that, though the public clamours for a message in poetry, it is angry when it gets it. But what words can describe its righteous rage when the poet, having preached his message, proceeds to translate it into action, as Tolstoi and d'Annunzio, for instance, attempted to do. A poet, too! Unpractical-and-all-that! For years d'Annunzio had preached in his novels the importance of being a leader of men, the importance of waiting for your moment and then acting swiftly.

In France and Italy, however, the people are simple and unafraid, still cherishing that respect for a poet which must have come down from the time when prophet, historian, and poet were one. Worldly possessions have never taught them to despise gifts of the mind or spirit. There is no rage against that extinct monster the "high-brow" —a poet has there no shame in avowing his profession and is not subject to the witticism of revue writers or red-nosed comedians. On the contrary, even in hotels in Italy, the servants respect rather than despise a writer, refraining for his sake from making the especial clatter that would greet his working in England. To a chiropodist one's trade actually may be confessed without fear of extra pain. Thus once, in Venice, I sat with my foot, sore and distressed, balanced on the knees of a mop-haired individual, who was beginning to brandish his razor. I had not wholly shaken off my English shyness at being a poet; but when suddenly asked my profession, reassured by the signed photograph of d'Annunzio hanging on the wall, I pulled myself together and answered boldly "Poet." "And I, too," he replied proudly, flourishing the steel blade and thumping himself on the chest as if it were a drum! Then my foot lay neglected as he declaimed some ten poems in the Venetian vernacular, or explained how little time he had in which to write—how, on Sundays, he would hide away the glittering insignia of his office, lock the door of the diminutive room and write sonnets. He told me, too, that he found his rather unpleasant trade an actual inspiration to him in the contrast it afforded between the material and spiritual. Ought I to chant my poems back to him, I wondered (and if so, how many?), or would that merely call down on my head—or, rather, on my foot—another shower of meteoric images, another spate of rhetoric? Still it was painful for me to think how, if ever the operations to my foot were completed, I must break down this fraternisation with hard ugly questions as to the cost of these material labours. But he was an artist, and understood. No payment would he accept from a brother poet—only a present, given of free will.

It is important to understand this respect felt for a poet in some foreign countries, as it helps to explain the degree of success to which d'Annunzio attained in his exploits. Not our most patriotic poet, not Mr Kipling himself, could ever raise a troop of boy-scouts for a war, far less an army corps! For in England the arts are despised, except for their monetary value, or as a new sensation for jaded appetites. The poet is here on the level of a hairdresser. Both are "artistic." D'Annunzio, a genius of European fame, a world figure, was written of in the Anglo-Saxon Press as if he were Jack-the-Ripper; while, on the other hand, poor Mrs Thompson, of the Thompson-Bywaters case, on the strength of her having mentioned, in a rather unfortunate letter to Bywaters, a book called *Bella Donna*, by Mr Robert Hichens, was interviewed by a representative of one of the cheaper Sunday journals

GABRIELE D'ANNUNZIO

Fiume and d'Annunzio

as to her opinion of the literary merits of *If Winter Comes* (which, incidentally, she considered a fine book, full of poetry, though the "loose moral tone of it" shocked her very much); and it is the considered opinion of many that, if the poor woman had not been most cruelly hanged, she would now be one of our best known, respected, and respectable of literary critics!

Yet if, as a nation, we remain unimpressed by poets, we might at least try to understand politics, which are our pride. If we deride and abuse d'Annunzio for being a poet, we might, surely, respect him as being one of the few men who, having brought his country into a terrible war, yet felt a certain responsibility. D'Annunzio by his reputation, as a writer of genius, a credit to the nation that produced him, and by his exceptional powers of oratory, brought Italy into the war on the side of the Allies. At least, then, those who admired the war should admire d'Annunzio—for persuading Italy to enter it, for the great personal bravery he displayed, and for the inspiration that this courage gave to his countrymen. But, having incurred this heavy moral liability, d'Annunzio was soon made to feel that he had brought the Italians into the war under false pretences; because, while secret treaties between England, France, and Italy guaranteed the latter certain territories if the Allies won, these treaties were not recognised by President Wilson, and have never been carried out. And it was this feeling of being accountable, this belief that Italy had come out of the war on a par with the defeated Powers, that made the poet risk his life once again at Fiume.

ii

The harsh north wind with the Greek name blew down the hard streets of Trieste; the electric light failed, perhaps as a fresh tribute to the anarchist Malatesta; and the fur-capped, flat-faced peasants huddled together in the great draughty station, speaking outlandish tongues.

No one knew quite when the train would start for Fiume, or at what hour it would arrive. Italian officers, Arditi, and Wolves of Tuscany gesticulated in groups outside the obsolete train. Cloaks, daggers, and the feathers of eagles proclaimed, rather melodramatically, that the Roman Legions were assembling once more under a new Cæsar. The flowing black ties of the Arditi declared that the new Cæsar was also, and obviously, a poet. It was a strange mixture of efficient militarism, high ideals, and a somewhat theatrical *vie de Bohème*, but there flickered, like flame, through the noisy, rapid chatter, an enthusiasm that had died out of the other poor and war-worn nations of the West.

The groups broke up and settled themselves

noisily in the carriages, and we began our interminable journey over the stony, frozen hills.

There was no light in the carriages or the corridors, but as the train jolted on, higher into the hills, the snow outside threw a ghostly, almost green light on the faces within. The somewhat Jugo-Slav lady in the corner complained bitterly that the cause of Fiume was a massacre of the innocents, that its army was entirely composed of children. The officer next me was smuggling into the Regency two enthusiasts of sixteen years of age who insisted on joining the Legions. One of them told me that he had tried to get over the border a year before, but had been turned back by the Italians. Both were evidently caught in the magic net of d'Annunzio's words, and their pockets were heavy with speeches, prayers, and threats, which they had, at the cost of immense labour, copied out from the poet's books and manifestos. If they could not get through to Fiume on the train, they would walk over the mountains; and thousands of boys all over Italy would do the same. They flocked to the New Crusade from Sardinia and Sicily, from great towns like Milan and Naples, and from withered cities like Ferrara, Mantua, and Parma. But, besides enthusiasm, there was another reason for this exodus. At eighteen or nineteen years of age all Italian subjects are conscripted, and the more imaginative ones preferred to go earlier and of their own accord.

Discursions

Entering Fiume was no easy matter. The Allies gave little encouragement to their subjects, not wishing them to visit the place; the Italian Government particularly resented visitors going to Fiume; and the Government of the Regency of Carnaro itself objected, as strongly, to receiving foreigners while there was a shortage of food and other necessities. Journalists, especially, they disliked, since many foreign ones who had been received, and treated with the greatest kindness, had then published attacks of the most personal kind on their hosts.

After journeying for five hours, our own passport troubles began; and my time was taken up in proving that I was not Lord Curzon of Kedleston. The soldier suspected me. He could not read easily, but he could distinguish that name on my papers. He felt dimly that he had heard it before —Curzon—Curzon—he muttered angrily. Then his eye lighted on the motto "Let Curzon holde what Curzon helde," and as he repeated it to himself in broken English, the import of this democratic refrain gradually penetrated his mind. Why, it was Lord Curzon, the chief instrument, with Lloyd George, of English Democracy! and firmly, almost angrily, he informed me that Lord Curzon was *not* allowed to proceed.

However, after minutes that were hours had passed, with the help of a Tuscan Wolf (who had, luckily, shared my flask of wine on the cold

Fiume and d'Annunzio

journey), I disproved the allegation, defeated the innuendo, and was allowed to proceed on a journey that became increasingly a thicket of passports and questions.

At last, after many hours, we arrived at Fiume. Below us lay the huge empty docks and warehouses, that seemed in giant disproportion to the size of the town. The lights of d'Annunzio's fleet winked wickedly beneath. Some of these vessels had been captured by the poet's pirates ; others, like the *Dante*, the leviathan outline of which loomed up out of the obscurity, had deserted to him from the Italian Navy. In this very cold darkness the lights flickered threateningly like the eyes of marine monsters, while each sound was crystallised into a greater precision. A noisy animation and general vitality heralded us into a new land.

One of the arguments advanced for the seizure of Fiume was that the bay is Italian by "right of landscape." This, though it may sound rather fantastic, is true enough. It belongs to the same order as Genoa or Naples. With its spur of hills sinking into the opalescence of the far sea, and the quivering, misty outlines of the islands, the traveller feels that he is once more in Italy, whereas Trieste is a different and an alien bay.

The next day sparkled with cold and sun. Outside the hotel is the chief piazza, where the Governor has placed two flagstaffs derived from those of Venice. And in the piazza itself loitered

Discursions

a crowd, surely more fantastic than any ever sheltered by the bubbles of St Mark. Every man seemed to wear a uniform designed by himself; some wore beards and had shaven heads like the Commander, others cultivated huge tufts of hair, half-a-foot long, waving out from their foreheads, and a black fez at the back of the head. Cloaks, feathers, and flowing black ties were universal, and all carried the "Roman dagger"; and among this young and swaggering throng walked two veterans, in Garibaldian uniform, with red waistcoats and long white hair.

An officer had been detailed to take us round, to show us the people, the army, and the town. He was gay, enthusiastic, pleasure-loving; London, more particularly—London, which he had never visited—was the object of an almost passionate longing : he dreamt of the tubes and motor-buses (for, in his way, he was a Futurist, though not a full-fledged one), the dazzling lights, the cars and theatres. And the buildings must be so beautiful, he thought. I replied, "Yes, some of them are fine, but none finer than the palaces and churches in Italian towns"; to which remark he returned a surprised query—"*Ma . . . il Palazzo del Crystol?*" And under this transcendental title it did, indeed, sound so beautiful, that I was loath to tell him that almost alone of London's population I appreciated it, and, at that, only because I possessed a literary and historical sense.

Fiume and d'Annunzio

This officer told me a story which helped to illustrate the Italian point of view about Fiume. Before the town was seized by d'Annunzio, after his aeroplane-ride from Venice, it was occupied by various detachments of Allied troops. This was bitterly resented in any case, both by the Italian officers quartered there and by the Italian population. But to make matters worse, one detachment of French troops consisted of negroes!

One night an Italian officer seeing a drunken negro leaning against the wall insulting the passers-by, went up to him and said: "What are you doing? Why are you here?" And the smiling black lips replied thickly, "*Pour la Civilisation!*"

The army of the Regency could be divided roughly into three parts: the first and biggest division consisted of Italian Romantics and Patriots, spiritual grandchildren of Garibaldi, gathered by the glamour of the Regent's name and words. Next in number were the Futurists, who, while disapproving of d'Annunzio as a writer, acclaimed him as a leader who took no heed of yesterday or for the morrow. Thirdly, closely allied to the Futurists, were the professional soldiers, who definitely preferred war to peace.

It is possible to illustrate these divisions by extreme cases. We met an officer, a great friend of d'Annunzio, who was a poet and refused to accept pay for his services. To the second division belonged Keller the Futurist, a bearded giant somewhat resembling Augustus John in appearance, who flew over Rome and pelted the venerable Giolitti's Ministry with beetroot. This act was acclaimed by the Press as "Futurist gesture by Keller." Thirdly, we met a man like a tiger, covered with medals instead of stripes; he was a Sardinian who had been imprisoned for murder but was released by the Italian Government, so it was said, at the outbreak of war, on condition that he promised to devote himself to slaying the enemy. He took thirty Austrian prisoners, and is reported to have strangled them with his own hands. This individual, however, was extremely shocked by the doings of the "Black-and-Tans" in Ireland, and smashed an empty champagne bottle—just behind our heads —as a protest.

Thus, in a curious way, d'Annunzio united idealists with criminals, and joined those who love the past of Italy with those who hate it. Some were drawn to him by the idea of a new Roman Empire, mighty in arms; others by the fervour of his words and the glamour of dead cities like Venice and Ravenna; while the Futurists, who agreed with Marinetti in thinking Venice a city of dead fish and decaying houses, inhabited by a people of waiters and touts, saw in d'Annunzio's policy the means of making Italy a great and insolent Power, with cement houses, great music-halls, and an efficient train service—an ideal since inherited from them by Mussolini.

Fiume and d'Annunzio

In spite of what we were told by the English Press, Gabriele d'Annunzio was, and is, and will remain, the idol of Young Italy. When he rode out into the stony country-side, the people, were they Italian or Croat, strewed the ground with flowers. In England, if d'Annunzio was mentioned, someone immediately asked, "Is he mad?" But to the Italians, a simple people, unused to the high moral tone, stern eloquence, and political sanity of a Lloyd George, oblivious to the subtleties of Lord Curzon and Sir Alfred Mond, or to the prophetic qualities of Messrs Winston Churchill and Bottomley, d'Annunzio remains a patriot and a great poet. To them he is the man who has done more for the Italian language than any writer since Dante, and the patriot who, alone, stood out against the futilities of the Peace Conference. Finally — and it is a popular claim in Italy—he is supposed to have been the cause of the fall of President Wilson, whom d'Annunzio referred to as "that cold-hearted maniac who sought to crucify Italy with nails torn from the German Chancellor of the Scrap of Paper."

We walked slowly up the steep hill, built in the well-known late Renaissance style of any Municipal Council—for it had been formerly the Town Hall. Inside there was a large, square, pillared hall, which d'Annunzio's exotic imagination had filled with pseudo-Byzantine flower-pots containing palms, and where soldiers lounged and typists rushed furiously in and out. Above are four galleries, and leading from the one nearest the sea were the closely guarded rooms of the poet. Sometimes for eighteen hours at a stretch he remained shut up in his apartment, refusing to see anyone. And in the hall below we spent two days of an incredible monotony, broken only by a two-hours' lecture on the political situation of the Regency, delivered by the Foreign Minister. This gentleman had the unique distinction of being the only bore in Fiume. Though this was well known there, he allowed us to find it out for ourselves. In appearance he belonged to the mustachioed, tactical-authority type; and while we balanced in agonised positions over diminutive maps, he laid down the law in that flowery French, reinforced with a twang like a guitar, which is the official language of so many Italians. But at the end of two hours we were informed that the Commander would receive us the next day. At five o'clock the following evening we were shown into d'Annunzio's private apartment. The room was a fairly large one, with little furniture, and with walls almost entirely covered with banners. On the inner side, supported by brackets, stood two gilded Saints from Florence, whose calm eyes gazed out over the deepening colour of the Fiumian Sea. On one of the tables near the fireplace stood a huge fifteenth-century bell—made by the great bell-maker of Arbe, and presented by that

Fiume and d'Annunzio

island to the Regent.   On the centre table were many papers and a pomegranate (d'Annunzio's symbol).   He was dressed in khaki, covered with ribbons, and on his left shoulder he wore the Italian Gold Medal for Valour, equivalent or superior to our Victoria Cross.   Though he was completely bald, with only one eye, nervous and tired, yet at the end of a few seconds one felt the influence of that extraordinary charm which has enabled him to change howling mobs into furious partisans.

As no description can ever conjure up so closely before readers the appearance of a man as a comparison to some other person with whose face they are familiar, it may interest music-lovers to be told that d'Annunzio very much resembles Stravinsky.

First the poet talked of England, of his admiration for Shelley (whose death himself tried to imitate at the age of fifteen in the Bay of Castellamare), of sport, and of the English greyhounds "running wild over the moors of Devonshire." There was not a little of absurdity to barbarian ears in his discourse, but through it there ran the thread of his extraordinary eloquence and fascination. We asked him to talk of Ireland, but, with a true feeling of hospitality for his guests, he refused. Instead, he told us of Fiume, of his great loneliness there; of how he, who loved books, pictures, and music, had remained there for fifteen months surrounded by peasants and soldiers, and of how

Discursions

the Italian Government, relying on his roving temperament, were trying to "bore him out."

We heard of the reckless enthusiasm of his legionaries, and how difficult it was to keep them at peace. Weary of waiting for battle, they must fight one another, and in a sham contest it was no unusual thing for there to be many serious casualties from bombs and bullet wounds. In his Proclamation of the Fiumian Constitution, d'Annunzio announced that music was to be "the religious and social institution of the Regency of Carnaro." Shortly after this he invited Toscanini, the eminent conductor, to bring his orchestra over from Trieste and give a series of concerts. It is related that the Governor organised one of these fights for the orchestra to witness. Four thousand troops, among whom were the two Garibaldian veterans, one aged seventy-eight and the other eighty-four, took part, and one hundred men were seriously injured by bombs. The orchestra, which had been playing in the quieter intervals, dropped their instruments—fired by a sudden enthusiasm—charged, and captured the trenches. Five of them were badly hurt in the battle!

We questioned the Governor about his seizure of the two islands in the bay, of which the hostile Press has made so much capital. These two small islands were handed over to Jugo-Slavia by the "Treaty of Rapallo," but the inhabitants, who were mostly Croat, came to him and asked to be annexed. They said they did not mind to whom they belonged, but they must belong to the same country that governed Fiume, otherwise they would lose their trade and starve.

D'Annunzio told us also of the strange conversations which he held with the people from his balcony. When a crowd assembled, he would go out and ask them what they wanted; someone would answer, and gradually a direct intercourse would thus be built up between the people and their ruler. This he claimed to be the first example of direct communication since Greek times. Several of these conversations have been printed and are extremely interesting to read.

As we left this Land of Youth the next day we observed our two friends, the Garibaldian veterans, making a simple but hearty meal of oysters, crayfish that looked like aeroplanes, and cherry-brandy—the staple if somewhat exotic foods of this strange country.

iii

Within six weeks of our departure from the Regency, d'Annunzio and his regime had fallen. The crafty old Minister, Giolitti, waited until the night before Christmas Eve. No newspapers would appear for three days in Italy; the Italian people would be without any information of his action throughout Christmas Eve, Christmas Day, and Boxing Day. He then sent the fleet to Fiume, with a threat to bombard the place to pieces if the poet remained there. D'Annunzio had always relied on the fact that feeling in Italy was so strongly in his favour that no Government would dare to oppose him in this open way. But now there was only one thing to be done—to leave Fiume, otherwise the defenceless inhabitants would be exposed to all the horrors of a severe naval bombardment. Some of the English and American papers accused the poet of cowardice in leaving the town. But it is hardly likely that this frail little genius, who had faced death hundreds of times in battle, who had flown over the Austrian Fleet and destroyed two vessels, who had flown over Vienna and the most perilous of battle-fields, would let his courage desert him now. D'Annunzio is one of the few men living who can afford to despise a charge of cowardice.

The whole affair was over before the Italian people were aware that it had begun. If they had heard, they would have stopped it. In all parts of Italy, when the news spread, theatres and shops were closed as a sign of popular mourning. But it was too late for public opinion to be of any value.

Meanwhile Fiume is still a problem, and d'Annunzio, far from being reviled in Italy, has just been presented with the ex-Kaiser's villa at Frascati by the Fascisti. In the peace of that

THE OLD THEATRE, BAYREUTH

Fiume and d'Annunzio

beautiful house and garden, or at Gardone, he lives in retirement, seeing his principles, defeated on a small scale at Fiume, conquer on a large scale in his own country.

The rather pitiful end of the poet's adventure was hailed with relief by our Press. It was supposed to finish "an awkward incident"; while the poet himself, for whom no words had been too good when his eloquence made Italy enter the war, was now abused and insulted under the idea that there could be no harm in kicking a man when he was down. One of the papers that rule our destinies published an article on him, headed "Chorus Girls and Champagne." When the intelligent writer of it thought d'Annunzio had time for these amusements we do not know, for the poet worked, as has been stated before, eighteen hours a day, and allowed himself little relaxation. The ingenuous author then proceeded to say that one could tell, "by the glassy glitter of d'Annunzio's snake-like eye," that he was addicted to the cocaine habit! This compelled us to write a letter to the journal pointing out that this "glassy glitter" was not due to drugs, but to the fact that his eye was a glass one, d'Annunzio having lost his own on behalf of the Allied Peoples, among whom the proprietor of the paper and the writer of the article were numbered.

Part iv
Teutonic Variations

i

Sentiment and Beauty

IT could, we think, be maintained that no beautiful building — that is to say, a fully-developed architectural entity as pleasing to the eye as any other work-of-art—was possible until the Age of Defence was over. In medieval times effort was necessarily deflected into the making of abbeys, cathedrals, and monasteries, these being the only buildings immune from attack; for in those days, curiously enough, it was forbidden to destroy or deface any holy edifice. Yet most of such structures in Northern Europe have a grim, fortress-like air, inseparable from any work of the time in cold latitudes. When, through huge formidable portals, you reach the forbidding interior, the feeling asserts itself that you are seeking sanctuary, that a man in armour is waiting for you with dagger or bludgeon outside—and it may even be a subconscious realisation, on the part of modern architects and clergymen, of this revengeful quality, so appropriate to the reading of the Old Testament, in these vast relics of a vendetta age, that has led to our newer churches being built in an Adulterated Gothic style.

As to houses erected in the Middle Ages, the

position was obviously a difficult one. If, when making for yourself a dwelling, it was necessary to consider, not whether it would be a convenient or beautiful one, but if the placing and construction of it were those best adapted for casting boulders or boiling oil—or both—upon the heads of your assailants, it was, from the beginning, more likely to become a picturesque ruin than a suitable or pleasing residence. Houses built thus —castles as they are called—belong essentially to the Stone Age, whatever our medievalists may say to the contrary: they are merely more convenient caves for a cleverer, more ferocious, troglodyte. At their best, they have the same beauty, neither more nor less, that is to be found in their modern equivalents—the battleship, submarine and tank—an unintentional beauty arising from a certain look of efficiency, from, in fact, their being so obviously suited to their purpose. Perhaps in the course of time these ruins achieve other accidental effects of beauty—clinging ivy or lichen-stained stone—a parasitic loveliness which is a help to those possessing a romantic turn-of-mind. Or, again, a Turneresque sunset, together with certain expected Walter-Scott-Wardour-Street details, will endear them to all old English spinsters who contracted the water-colour habit during a visit to Italy—a short sojourn in Rome, Florence or Naples—in their young days.

But, quite apart from the actual though necessary

Sentiment and Beauty

ugliness of houses designed to withstand warfare, it is obvious that if a man insists on spending his fortune on flint implements (though these were cheap enough), Greek fire, boiling oil, wrought iron cannon, or even on that acme of modern convenience, the tank, he will be able to spend less on the beautifying of his home. It may be that money is now better laid out, from the point of view both of æsthetics and political economy, in creating a tank than in building the garden city which, in the end, that tank will most certainly destroy. But it was not always thus.

When civilisation was making a fresh start in the Western world, it was amid the peace of the Venetian lagoons that there rose up the most lovely palaces in Europe. Here was no necessity for defence; no enemy could enter this watery fastness to burn or destroy. Happy in the amphibious character of his city, the Venetian merchant need not consider his mansion as a fortress, but could build with convenience and beauty for his only objects. He could spend the money with which in other countries it would have been necessary to purchase a stock of armour—cross-bows, clubs, rapiers, bludgeons, oil (for boiling, not for giving light), stone slings, stone balls, instruments of torture and Greek fire—on the enriching of his home. He could encrust the façade with slabs and strips of marble, split so as to give the pattern of a brocade, divide it with marble pillars, clustered together and bearing capitals of carved stone, inlay it with bosses of porphyry, serpentine, or bas-reliefs which his fleet had stolen from the dying Eastern Empire, with no fear that these things would be burnt or smashed. If he were too poor to indulge in these extravagances he could paint the outside of his house in stripes, checks, and gay patterns, with no thought of their being immediately obliterated. But in almost every other European city at this period the money spent thus would have been directed into making the living-rooms as small, the walls as thick, the front as stern as possible. Yet these light-hearted Venetian palaces are more beautiful than their frowning, yellow contemporaries at Florence or Siena, and have outlived the fifty-foot thick walls of Heidelberg, Kenilworth or Windsor.

Domestic architecture began early, too, in Palermo, where, blessed by its guardian sea and by the rule of wise kings, there was an efflorescence unequalled except at Venice.

But in England the building of beautiful houses can hardly be said to have begun until the Wars of the Roses were ended. Gradually the grim character of the Gothic altered : the heavy buttress took to itself wings and flew ; the early intentions of fortification were forgotten, took on a merely ornamental value. Often, when something originally intended for war, for attack or defence, sinks

Sentiment and Beauty

into a forgetful old age, it assumes a certain beauty. The rhinoceros, clumsy and grotesque as the armoured knight, becomes transformed into the gracious unicorn. The savage butting horn of the one becomes the fruit-transfixing ivory of the other. In the same way you find Knole, or the early part of Hampton Court, springing out of the forbidding ruins of a feudal castle. But after that, even, comes the greatest period of English domestic architecture, so well exemplified in Wilton House and Bolsover Castle, only, alas! to be cut short in its best, most typical phase by the outbreak of the Civil War, which was to warp its tradition for ever. While in Germany, owing to the warlike character of the reigning princes and great nobles, domestic building achieved little but accidental—or romantic—beauty until the latter half of the seventeenth century. Thus, naturally, since she began her triumph at so late an age, Germany is particularly rich in palaces and churches of the Baroque and Rococo periods.

It is curious how little is heard of these in England. Versailles is known universally, though still perhaps more wondered at than admired by the sober English taste; but the very sound of Sans Souci and the New Palace at Potsdam, both really admirable of their kind, to English ears still suggests some form of absurdity, so inseparably is the word Potsdam—even more than Versailles—connected with the rise of Militarism in Europe:

and to us fortunately, except during wars, there has always been something comic about the strutting boastfulness of great armies. To the wealth of palaces, painted rooms, and formal gardens in Southern Germany, this significance is lacking; yet little is heard of them.

In Southern Germany it is, of course, that the best rococo work is to be found; for it should be recognised that this style was Catholic in its invention and inspiration, Jesuitical in its faults, and is, in reality, only to be found at its best in Catholic countries. Thus, though the eighteenth century was a great period for building in England, little rococo work is to be discovered there. We had achieved a more solid, a Protestant style, to be seen at its best in Houghton and Holkham. Yet there are traces of the rococo in other English arts—Pope for instance is the most perfect rococo artist we possess; and in order to understand, to appreciate fully his work, it is necessary to remember that he was a Papist.

Even before the "great" war had come to make it an article of faith, German art — apart from German music—was suspect to us. For to the untravelled Englishman it suggested the vagaries of the Prince Consort's taste—tartan carpets, over-gilded furniture, antlers, the Crystal Palace, and cairngorms; while the English who knew Germany (again we are not talking of musicians) could be divided roughly into three groups: Firstly there were those who admired Berlin as the perfect modern city, were taken in by all the second-rate glitter, thought the Kaiser the summit of European society, and were thrilled by the square-heads and rattling sabres of his army. Secondly there were those people now scornfully referred to, we believe, as "high-brows"—that is to say, learned men and women studying education and housing, and certainly too busily engaged in the difficult, almost dangerous task of trying to awaken an enthusiasm for these subjects among their countrymen, to have any time left over for the study of art of any period. Thirdly appear those arty-crafty folk who visited Germany to see Nüremberg and Rothenburg, seriously admiring black-and-white houses clustered together, glaring down into gloomy, factory-fed rivers, or instruments of torture, iron-virgins and their like, seeing in them not the ancestors of Big-Bertha and gas-shell, but merely dear, decorative bits of old wrought-iron. These arty, very crafty people, though perhaps really interested in art, were so nourished on Pre-Raphaelite milk, that they would never question the doctrines of William Morris or Ruskin, never even spare a glance for the later palaces of Germany.

In spite of their learning and enthusiasm for things of the mind, in spite or perhaps because of their genius for music, it is probable that the Germans have always had a stronger streak of barbarism in their natures than is to be found in the French, English, or Italians. They never enjoyed to the same degree as these peoples the advantage of a Roman foundation. But it was the triumph of the latter half of the seventeenth and, above all, of the eighteenth century, to force, for the first time since the passing of the Roman Empire, an elegant, if somewhat artificial, culture upon the ruling classes in nearly every country. Libraries, museums, and picture galleries suddenly appeared everywhere. Palaces sprang up like gilded mushrooms in one night all over the world—in Italy, France, Spain, England, Poland, Mexico, Russia, and Germany; and, though these palaces might lack the qualities of the greatest art, could never attempt to rival the earlier ones at Venice, Urbino, Mantua, or Rome, they were, at least, the pleasure-houses of civilised beings.

And the contribution of Germany to this culture was an important one. The conditions there, indeed, were very favourable. As in Italy, the necessary stimulus was found in the competition of numerous small courts, but these were less cramped by poverty, less embarrassed by being already in the possession of magnificent homes. Thus kings, grand dukes, prince-bishops, margraves, were all engaged in a titanic but harmless warfare to proclaim their respective wealth and importance; seas of cement, mountains of brick and stone, whole valleys of rare marble, and, in Russia, quarries even of amethyst, malachite, and onyx, oceans of gilding were the fuel for these rich battles. It was a world-wide sequel to the Field of the Cloth-of-Gold. Perhaps the ambition, which, to put it frankly, was the desire to "show off," may have been a mean one; but at any rate the manner was worthy. Our plainer, less ambitious statesmen achieve the same object by the threat of a new war in the Near East, or by the addition of several shillings to the Income Tax (latterly during the war the largeness of our direct taxation became obviously even a source of pride); but if this money were spent in the creation or buying of a work-of-art, it would be recognised as wicked extravagance— and no lives would be lost! The same age which conceives and executes Dreadnoughts at the cost of eight or nine million pounds each, which special- ises in tank and big gun, sees Stowe, a more beautiful but almost equal extravagance, nearly perish for lack of funds. In Germany, too, the palaces are doomed; the plaster is falling in mimic snowstorms; in the gardens the trees have been cut, and in most of them the fountains have ceased playing for ever:

> "An other age shall see the golden ear
> Imbrown the slope and nod on the parterre."

At first the Germans, distrusting their own power, made use of foreign artists and workmen. In this manner they learnt much, and, out of the

Discursions

knowledge thus acquired, developed, perhaps, for the first time, a national style. This latter is seen at its best in the beautifully dignified work of J. B. Neumann of Würzburg, who designed the Concordia at Bamberg (one of the most lovely smaller houses in Germany), worked on the palace there, and designed the still more magnificent one in his native town, of which we write elsewhere. He and his school gave to their work a strength, richness, and solidity, both of material and construction, which was lacking in the flimsier, more fantastic improvisations of Italy, Sicily, and Spain.

From the Margrave's Window

ARRIVING at Bayreuth after dark, little is visible of the town—nor can one even see "The Wagner Theatre and large lunatic asylum on the right" which Baedeker tactfully indicates together, as being "conspicuous." Walking through the black, ill-lighted streets, busy disentangling our luggage from some form of boy-scout or local-black-hand demonstration, no thought came to us of the beauty of our surroundings. We were prepared for a charming old town, but not for the perfection we found here.

To many English people Bayreuth suggests only the image of a monstrous theatre in a pine-wood, of music-lovers, dark and beaked like harpies, hastily swallowing doughnuts and gulping down hot chocolate in the *entr'actes* before they return to wallow once more in the luxuriance and fertility of Wagner's genius. But though the fame of that great composer is linked inseparably with Bayreuth, the town itself belongs to another period— one as divorced in ideas from the music and drama of Wagner as is possible to imagine—an unheroic epoch of miniature courts and polite learning, and of passions well ordered; a time in which everyone but the highwayman observed certain rules of order, deportment, art, and even of love, but a world, all the same, in which already lurked those germs of revolution which were to destroy it artistically and politically. Not only were these germs allowed, they were actually encouraged. And in this small town, under the same roof as the Court, lived for some time one of the chief destroyers of his own age, though the creator of innumerable other ones, Voltaire! This town, then, belongs more to the time of Voltaire than of Wagner; it is of one predominant style in detail and planning, as is Bath (most delightful of English cities), with the addition—and it is one that no perfect town can afford to neglect — of a derelict palace that strangers can visit at any hour. Outside Bayreuth, too, there is another royal residence, half-cottage, half-palace, set back three miles in the country among golden cornfields and hanging woods.

Most of the architectural background here was conceived between the years 1700 and 1760; much of it inspired by that remarkable woman the Margravine Sophie-Wilhelmine, sister of Frederick the Great, and friend of Voltaire. She it was who imported from Paris a certain French architect, St Pierre; and he lived here for many years, building at least half the town. Churches, palaces, orangeries, gardens, convents, all sprang into being at a touch of his magic wand; while he laid out the town itself in formal but commodious fashion. Yet the effect is always German, not French—a tribute to the good sense and understanding of an architect who must have comprehended that a style unsuited to its neighbourhood could no more be imposed upon a town than foreign rule upon the inhabitants.

In the centre of the town is the New Palace, an admirable low building of two storeys, designed by St Pierre for Frederick, husband of Wilhelmine. Most palaces built at this date consisted of but two storeys, for at Versailles Louis XIV. had started the idea that he was too important to have people sleeping, or even walking, above him; an idea welcomed with great enthusiasm by the mimic monarchs and small rulers of the German States. This residence is a charming one, sufficiently impressive yet not pompous, a comfortable country house brushed up for the occasion, situated in a square built of the same soft grey stone, in the same epoch and, presumably, by the same architect.

Set up in the middle of this square, for all to see, is a fountain bearing an equestrian statue of Margrave Christian Edward, a rather distinguished general and Marshal of the Empire. But here he rides in surpassing pomp. Beneath a plumed helmet, his periwig flows in lava-like curls over his breastplate; his face, with its strongly-marked rococo features, full of character, has the severe expression that distinguishes the less objectionable Roman Emperors. Sword hanging from one hand,

Discursions

Marshal's baton gripped in the other, he is obviously ready for any fray, were it not that his horse's victorious career is being checked by the uplifted fist of a favourite dwarf. The latter is wearing that kilt or abbreviated toga which seems to have been the conventional court-dress for black dwarfs of the period. At the base of the fountain are shown the Four Quarters of the Globe, proclaiming the Margrave's martial prowess and civil virtues in full - throated chorus. The American Indian, with high-feathered head-dress (how seldom one sees a sculptured Red Indian), is particularly enthusiastic in this vociferation, though one is inclined to doubt whether many natives of that continent were, in reality, aware of the Margrave's conquests. This fountain is an enchanting and grotesque work-of-art, having something of the quality which Aubrey Beardsley introduced into his drawings for *The Rape of the Lock*.

The interior of the New Palace is comparatively disappointing, though it contains much beautiful furniture and some fine panels of Brussels tapestry. The garden front is low, rambling, comfortable-looking, but has only one real architectural feature : a balcony which, supported by two giant satyr-caryatides, bellies out over the garden. Detached from the body of the palace is a pavilion that, though much smaller, rather resembles Devonshire House. The interior is full of beautiful plaster-work such as is found, carried out by Venetian

MARGRAVE'S PALACE, BAYREUTH

artists, all over Europe—very much like the two drawing-rooms in the now derelict Sutton-Scarsdale in Derbyshire ; work of a wonderful fineness, executed by a Venetian, Martino Petrozzi, who, working under St Pierre, decorated the interior of the royal church as well as many rooms in the palace.

The garden is rather small, but has that ideal beauty, melancholy yet kindly, which one noticed as a child in old gardens. Here are statues, formal canals, and cut hedges of yew ; but the general effect is not overwhelming, as is sometimes that of the larger gardens of this rather heartless century. This pleasant palace and garden, unpretentious yet in a way imposing, comfortable, and obviously the home of nice people (we heard the Doge's Palace described, the other day, as the Unpleasant Home of Unpleasant People), would not have incurred the wrath of Pope as did those vast machines which he compares to Brobdingnag.

" Who but must laugh, the master when he sees,
  A puny insect shivering at a breeze !
  Lo, what huge heaps of littleness around !
  The whole a laboured quarry above ground.
          .   .   .   .   .   .

  The suffering eye inverted Nature sees,
  Trees cut to statues, statues thick as trees."

The thick-boled elms with their golden leaves, doubled by the flat sheets of water mirroring all the intricate arrangements of branches, twigs, and sky, the long untended grass heavy with dew, the

Discursions

statue with its rustic, rather clumsy, grace, set on a little island, all have a sympathy which is lacking in the portentous array of Versailles or Nymphenberg: here the effect is out of all proportion to the work, for little labour was necessary, little money was spent, on the creation of this garden. The house lies long and low behind you. The high red-brick walls of the orchards are soft coloured, covered with the flat branches, clutching at the walls like open fingers, of pear and plum tree. The flowers in the beds, many-coloured and tall, are just conscious of the winter so soon to come. The purples, pinks, and deep reds are as bright yet soft as ever, but the full green stalks and thick leaves are touched with brown, and have too much moisture on them, whether of rain or dew, dripping, if you touch them, with little silver bells. There is a dampness in the air, a misty scent, rather sad but still fresh and sweet, of decaying leaves and overblown flowers, though in a day or two the dry aromatic smell of a bonfire will lie sharply on the rain-washed air, and the ground will be hard and silvered with the grip of winter.

From the palace all the streets are laid out regularly—stone houses, well built, with pillars of cut stone; balconies made for hot summer nights, and high roofs, alternate with gate-piers, crowned with trophies and coats-of-arms. These, like the palace, and the church which lies hidden away in the Old Palace, are by St Pierre. This Old

From the Margrave's Window

Palace is a rather uninspired building, but the royal church, though not beautiful outside, has a charming interior decorated with plaster-work by Petrozzi.   Over the walls and ceilings a mob of insubordinate Cupids are engaged in whirling away with the Cardinal's hat, trying on the Bishop's mitre, and even, we regret to say, stealing the keys from St Peter.   All this work is in relief, but lies very flat against the wall and is exquisitely designed.

The chief monument of the French architect, though, is undoubtedly the Hermitage, the Margravine Sophie Wilhelmine's summer resting-place, a palace complete — replete even — "with every modern convenience" of that age — sun - temple, water - basin, pebble - work orangery, shell - work grotto, fountain, mirror-room, Chinese decoration, Roman amphitheatre and pseudo-classical remains.

Autumn must be the ideal time for walking through these wide gardens; it tones down the general decay, making it merely a part of the usual yearly disintegration of Nature, while frosty sunshine still gives an aureole of golden leaves to the fountains which glitter like rockets in the cold air.   Only the sham ruins remain perfect and untouched in this desolation, immune from Time's decrees.   It is a curious perverse trait, full of ironic comment, this habit formed by artificial ruins, of remaining intact!   Our mind went back to the war, to the garden of an ugly château near Ypres, the former home of a rich manufacturer.

Discursions

When we remember it, trenches stretched away in hideous, angular lines beneath smashed monkey-puzzle-trees and dead, torn weeping-willows. The whole rank garden was full of bits and ends of things—of Greek temples, plaster statues, rustic summer-houses—while the former position of the château was marked by the gaping of broken cellars. Among all this refuse only one thing remained entire and invulnerable—a sham-Gothic ruin on an exposed little mound. Nothing could touch it. The proprietor had built it in January 1914. He wanted a ruin, he said. . . . If only he had been possessed of a little more patience . . . ! But nothing known to modern man could break down the monstrous resistance of that thing. It had been intended as a skeleton at the feast, and now was determined never to go down to the tomb.

So, at the Hermitage, the Roman amphitheatre and pseudo-classical remains are in perfect order, though the rest of the garden is perishing. But it is still beautiful, full of old trees, groups of statuary and the sound of flowing water. Under the tall elephant-coloured trunks of the beech-trees Tritons yet blow down their mossy conchs with an air of triumph. Interminable green tunnels stretch to an almost invisible blue stretch of country ; and entering one of these alleys is like gazing down the wrong end of a telescope, so distant, round and small is the view-point.

From the Margrave's Window

Placed among all these things is the Hermitage itself, where the little Royalties spent their thebaidic lives, like children who play at being Red Indians, surrounded by an array of marble banqueting-halls, mirror-rooms, plaster-orchards and a world of *chinoiserie*. Hermits were very popular just then. If you were an important person, but did not play at being one yourself, you employed a proxy who would live in the park. At one great house in England the accounts disclose a half-yearly payment of £300 to a hermit, who had, for this commensurate salary, to remain bearded and in a state of picturesque dirtiness for six months in the year, in an artificial cave at a suitable distance from the house, just far enough (but not too far) for the fashionable house-party, with its court of subservient poets and painters, to visit, walking there in the afternoons, peering into the semi-darkness with a little thrill of wonder and excitement. To go and see the hermit was, in fact, rather like a more intelligent form of golf. During the winter months, however, the anchorite was permitted to retire to a warmer, more congenial dwelling in the country town nearby, where, no doubt, he could live in some comfort upon his hardly-earned income.

The Hermitage here is half-cottage, half-palace. The exterior is fronted with stucco-rocks, to give it a wild, cave-like appearance. Even the chimneys are built of rockwork! The feast-hall, its most important room, is a large, handsome apartment panelled with marble, rather in the manner of some of the rooms at the Trianon. But the Margravine's writing-room is perhaps the most remarkable feature of the house; with a square alcove for a couch at one end, the whole expanse of wall and ceiling is covered entirely with angular, irregular patches of mirror, reflecting every object in a state of semi-consciousness—a very modern room that looks as if it had been designed by one of the French Cubists, showing (as some dignified critics write about certain modern poetry) "a striving to be original at all costs." Next-door to this is the music-room, as unusual but more beautiful in its decoration, and, again, very near to the modern feeling. The ceiling has on it in bas-relief a design of plaster Cupids playing huge 'cellos, while upon the walls, arranged in panels, are plaster still-lives of violins, bagpipes, flutes, mandolins and other musical instruments. These gilded trophies, once more by Martino Petrozzi, are, except for their being in plaster, curiously in the manner of Severini, Juan Gris, Picasso, and other modern artists.

The Chinese rooms, of which there are so many different examples in German palaces, are here made of panels torn from a Coromandel screen, while the ceilings are inlaid with squares of mirror, in whose watery light are reflected many dragons and Oriental beasts.

From the Margrave's Window

Near the Hermitage is the Orangery, an imposing semicircular building with an arcaded front, plastered with designs in pebble-work. Steps, curving with the façade, lead down in shallow flights to a large basin of water, where monsters rise out of the depths, spouting foam. The actual centre of the Orangery is an octagonal building with a domed roof, disconnected from the two curved wings. This is the Sun-Temple.

The colonnades shelter a series of rooms most typical of their period. There is to be found in them much beauty, but also a certain desire to startle and surprise. First comes a chamber hung with Chinese glass-paintings, the ceiling covered with mirror and painted with formal wreaths of flowers. Then follows a suite of rooms, containing every sort of plaster-work. We walk out into the air for a minute, then enter the Sun-Temple, a stately pavilion with marble walls and pilasters, very correct in manner and curiously unlike the rest of the decoration here. More Chinese rooms ensue, and then comes the most entertaining apartment of all. It is a large, square room, in the middle of which is a dolphin fountain, while each corner has a miniature grotto in it, with water dripping down in thin stalactites. The walls are divided by pilasters, covered with painted creepers, and crowned by large vases of painted flowers in relief, among which squat gaudy macaws and many tropical birds. There is a lattice-work dado; and above this, between the pillars, are orange-trees and peach-trees of painted plaster, offering you their false fruit with a very naturalistic air. When the doors are closed, country gates, with trees in the distance, take their place.

This amusing, fantastic pleasure-house, sheltered by the cool shadow of colonnades and high swaying branches, while ceiling and floor are dappled with circling patches of light thrice refined by their penetration through trees, arcades, and flowing water, must have made an ideal summer resting-place for the royal hermits. And no doubt the thin, rather acid shadow of M. Voltaire often rested with them here, though his spirit was laid like an axe at the base of these artificial trees of peach and orange.

Murray's *Guide to Southern Germany* of 1840 (and incidentally it is a much better guide-book than any we can now buy) has one lapse into un-conscious humour, when it describes the Orangery and Sun-Temple as being a copy of St Peter's at Rome! What exactly it means, alas! we shall never know. Perhaps it confounded the architect's name, St Pierre, with St Peter, and was finally led away by the curve of the twin arcades.

The country, out of which this park and garden are constructed, varies delightfully. Flat open spaces alternate with woods, sweeping down steep hills; and in the hollows, everywhere, are playing waters and green-stained statues, while at only a little

From the Margrave's Window

distance from the Orangery, but at a considerable
depth beneath it, is the Shell Grotto, which must
have been designed by some Venetian garden-
architect. It is a high, dark pavilion, its dome
shaped like a fruit, where masks peer blindly out
of the surrounding blackness, and monsters bend
their faces down to gaze in ours. Water gushes
from every place—from floor, wall, and ceiling—
giving a cool, cellar-like atmosphere more necessary
to the heats of Italy than to the German autumn.
An old woman came in, placing a crown or tiara,
upon which were six lighted candles, on the floor
beneath all these fluttering ribbons of water.
Suddenly there was the sound of an even greater
rushing of spray, and the crown ascended, as if
flying, twenty feet up into the air, supported on
a quivering pillar of foam. Certainly it is a great
moment when that solid tiara dances aloft,
gradually lighting the darkness, till the whole
mass of rising and falling water glistens as if a
rainbow had been caught fast, frozen in a cave
of crystal icicles; it shows how the eighteenth
century could achieve the impossible, reducing
life and even the elements to toys, and with
what magic it could balance an artificial culture
over forces still savage and untamed.

   •   •   •   •   •   •   •

The mention of a theatre at Bayreuth will,
doubtless, call up to English minds the image
of a huge, half-timbered barn in those dreary

Discursions

Aldershot-like pine-woods. But the Opera House in the town is as remarkable as the Wagnerian one, and much pleasanter to look at. Curiously enough it is the very symbol of everything Wagner fought against; it exemplifies all those rules of music and the theatre which, because they had become petrified in his time, because they were then utterly without life, it was Wagner's triumph to break down and destroy. But now, again, these things have life; their tyranny has been broken and the spirit has come back to them, while Wagner, perhaps, has put in their place laws equally stagnant and less patined with age.

Designed by Giuseppe Bibbiena, no more perfect example of the eighteenth-century opera house is to be found anywhere—not even in Italy, the home of the theatre. And though the Bibbiena family of Bologna—a family that was almost a tribe, so great its numbers—produced the most celebrated stage decorators of the time, with a world-wide reputation, yet comparatively few of its works survive. This Opera House, therefore, apart from any question of beauty, belongs to the history of the theatre: but, though it is a signed work, with the designer's name writ large over the Royal Box, no guide-book mentions that it is a Bibbiena creation.

The façade was planned by St Pierre, and is a stately, typically German, stone building, with its projection of three large doors. Above these several Corinthian pillars rise up to support a coved and orange-tiled roof, the cornice of which is set with eight stone statues. But this dignified, stolid front gives no hint of the lively Italian riot that is proceeding within. It is merely the heavy leather case for an intricate, fantastic piece of jewellery; for the interior is equal, in imaginative quality and execution, to any theatre-work of its time, is more beautiful even than the Phœnix at Venice or the San Carlo at Naples. Like them, the theatre is built up entirely out of opera-boxes, of which here there are only three tiers; while the most important architectural feature of the house, to which all things, even the stage, are subordinated, is the Royal Box, set in the middle and stretching from floor to roof. At the corners of the house, on either side above the stage, are two trumpeters' galleries, from which fanfares would sound into the gilded, candle-lit air upon the arrival of the Royal party. The doors would be thrown wide, and in they would walk, covered with miniature orders—golden eagles and fleeces, diamond stars and crosses, the chivalric badges of such Lilliputian States as Monaco, Luxembourg, and Bayreuth, while in virtue of the Margravine's relationship to Frederick, one or two of the most favoured may even sport a Prussian order. Immediately all eyes were fixed upon this box, the rival of the stage. So intense would be the

interest, that even the candles would stop flickering, as if to hold their breath at the mere sight of
so much glory. Little showers of white powder
would fall in miniature cascades through the golden
air from the curving ranges of boxes, as the ladies
and gentlemen moved their heads or shifted their
positions so as not to miss a single gesture or
expression of the Margrave and Margravine who
now entered their splendid cage. They sit down
next to each other in their huge, rococo chairs;
and the mummers, much impressed—respecting
competitors for the public interest, and ones who
possess the hereditary gift both of acting and
of holding the attention of the audience all the
time, however interesting or exciting may be the
rival spectacle on the stage proper—shine again
in the reflected glory of the Royal Box just
opposite them.   And how well the theatre-
designer of that time understood the mounting of
Royalty! There should always be a strong alliance
between State, Church, and Theatre. Even now
a judicious employment of stage designers might
restore fallen monarchies and strengthen the
existing ones; for, after all, the ritual of a State
function is intended to impress the crowd. Why
not, then, employ those who understand the business?   M. Diaghileff should direct a coronation,
Gordon Craig some more simple ceremonial, while
Mr Granville Barker ought to be put in charge of
one of the numerous Royal bazaars, converting it

THE OLD THEATRE, BAYREUTH.　INTERIOR

From the Margrave's Window

into a land of golden fairies. Mr Louis Napoleon Parker would mount admirably the Royal kick-off at a football match, while Royal marriages, which, to judge from the halfpenny papers, become more fairy-story-like, more Dick-Whittington-Aladdin-Cinderella-like every day, should, we think, be placed under the efficient control of Mr Arthur Collins. Think of the Big-Heads arriving at the Abbey like so many politicians! Think of Bakst's ogres and monsters! Then there are the more Twankey-like ceremonies, inspections of laundry and school-children. Who would present these best? They need a more simple artistry. But we are a nation of amateurs, and prefer the employment of a dilettante Lord Chamberlain to that of gentlemen who must necessarily understand the business better, both artistically and economically.

But in this theatre the Royal Box was admirably staged by Bibbiena, who understood the whole business as if born to it. Opposite the proscenium, in the centre of the house, a balustraded double staircase leads from it down to the plebeian floor. The box itself is a small painted room, on each side of which are two pillars with gilded vines, carrying bunches of grapes, twined round them; above is a canopy of painted wood, with large hanging gilded-wood tassels. Higher up, and slightly at the side, two Cupids arrange formal bouquets in two vast flower-vases. Then come

Discursions

two allegorical figures, threatened by a fierce eagle flapping his powerful gilded wings. Now tower up a huge crown, several Caryatides, and (we are at the top of the house) two flying Cupids, waving a rococo shield on which is inscribed "pro Friederiko et Sophia Josephus Gallus Bibbienna fecit, anno MDCCXLVIII." Opposite, over the stage, two huge flying figures are blowing fanfares in the direction of the Royal party.

The theatre is typical of the town. About the whole place there is that enchanting mock-heroic air which is illustrated in literature by Pope's *Rape of the Lock* — an atmosphere which still lingers only in such decayed German princely towns. Everywhere the palaces, churches, theatres, gardens, squares, even the very streets, are set for the strutting of these tiny figures, all engaged in striking the correct Sun-King attitude ; but there is something very beautiful as well as pathetic about this posturing. The cultivation of music, literature, and the arts is always noble, even if the ultimate aim is a little mean, the manner a little ostentatious. But here, in spite of bombast and rhetoric, is a comfortable, homely air—a sense that the Margraves themselves knew that it was only play ; a solidity together with a feeling of heart, to be found only in these small principalities, and very absent in the overwhelming grandeur of Versailles, the source from which all these things come.

iii

A German Garden

DRAWN up in the village street, outside a church that belonged to the country as much as any of the trees or cattle, the taxicab allowed us to escape from the throbbing horror of the German cities into the placid life of a wet afternoon in a small hamlet. The church bells rang with a gentle, tolling sound, kindly yet irritating, like the voice of a lady visitor in hospital or pauper ward; and every blade of grass blown back by the slight gusts of wind seemed laden with small, gently-ringing bells of silver that repeated the tolling in miniature. This rhythm of bells, trees, and even of grass, produced an atmosphere at once calm, peaceful, and melancholy. All at once the rhythm became broken, the wind stopped its playing, and "the blue pebbles of the rain" began to fall in earnest, beating up into little fountains and watery catherine-wheels at the sloping borders of the road. The afternoon was now sufficiently wet to be interesting, for, in the tattooing sound made by the rain as it drummed its watery fingers upon the various hard surfaces, it was possible to distinguish many tunes, played with a precision and sense of time that would do credit to any executant. But almost before one tune was finished, it would merge into another; and suddenly, before we were in the full swing of this new game imposed upon us, the music ceased and the blue pebbles lengthened into disappointing grey strings, dull and ugly.

It was at this moment of disillusionment that the geese hastily waddled into the village street, at once imparting that note of human interest previously lacking in the view from our window. In twos they came, as if possessing an inherited knowledge of a previous set of rainy days, and, indeed, strangely suspicious of the imminence of another ark. They waddled round, scanning road and gutter carefully, as you might see housewives marketing. Here was a bargain obviously, and they tapped eagerly on the stone border of the pavement with their yellow beaks, making a hard wooden sound, peering, as if to examine the durability of some material. Now they would turn away again, disappointed but still hopeful, hissing slightly with excitement at the damp, fat smells of the country-side, of grass, foliage, wet mould, haystacks, cabbages, and all those scents that are exhaled so strongly in humid air.

Faces now appeared at one or two of the windows in the street. The scene became almost familiar, so traditional was it — like one of those tinny, very realistic paintings by the elder Breughel, who is as true to the look of the people here as

A German Garden

Hogarth and Rowlandson are to the look of theirs, and who, at the same time, summed up the Flemish and German rustic quality as surely as George Morland represented the English one.   Down this very national perspective now marched a whole army of geese, led by a ragged girl whose flaxen hair and bright colouring proclaimed the nearness of her kin to the country-side, to the apples that still lie, rosy-red, high up on the golden branches of the fruit-trees which everywhere edge the roads —boughs hung with silvery cobwebs resembling the counterfeit hoar-frost on a Christmas tree—or to the yellow vines that grow here in so stiff and upright a way—not clinging in luxuriant wreaths, or touched with crimson as are the Italian ones. The goose-girl diminished into the distance at the head of her white army, and a cart came into sight dragged by two flax-coloured oxen, plodding peacefully along and driven by a large fair man in tattered clothing, while placed on his head was one of those old, round military-caps, the very shape and hue of which suggest an army of brutalised slaves, of dummies obeying some ferocious ventriloquist; a cap that must have witnessed many disasters, and woke in us horrid memories of bodies lying in queer, rigid attitudes among the burnt grass of dull brown plains.

The rain now drew aside its curtain, showing us for the first time the green-gold hills hanging above the town, and fields where rooks rose up and sank down in the air like pieces of charred paper lifted by the wind. Everything was bathed in light; each tree, each weed, each red brick in the street shone in air that was deceivingly transparent; brittle as glass it seemed, and yet somehow more tangible for its washing. The silver bells that we had seen trembling on leaf and grass blade were now silent, having arranged themselves in other shapes, glistening wreaths of crystal flowers or flaming geometric patterns such as are visible in the shifting masses of a kaleidoscope. Up the wet road to their homes went the geese in twos, no doubt laden with the rich spoil of a wet afternoon, and obviously scorning those disciplined sisters whose march up the road they had regarded with such marked disapproval. As they floated further away their bodies shone more brightly in this new light, till they seemed white-washed boats gently rocking on some watery surface.

Steeped in this stolid, peaceful life that must have lasted through countless centuries, it was possible for the first time for many days to forget for a while the tragedy of this blundering, tactless, over-obedient yet kindly people. How far away the cities seemed, with their over-heated restaurants and cabarets full of fur-clad harpies, each one of whom engrosses the food of about one hundred starving people a day! A paragraph appeared in *The Times*[1] a little time ago saying that

[1] This was written in 1922.

A German Garden

the financiers who understood the fluctuation in exchange values were now leaving Vienna in order to reside in Berlin, where their help and advice were much appreciated by the Prussian bankers who did not yet fully understand this business. The day of Vienna is over, then, and that of Berlin is beginning! They are quite unmoved, these birds of prey with their beaked, bird - like faces and beady eyes, guzzling and drinking, waiting till the hour strikes for them to move on, to drain the blood of the next victim. Like some warning figure, some horrible spectre of doom, they always appear a few months before the end. . . . Far away, too, seemed the factories, those that are idle and those others that work feverishly, the employees of which are paid enormous wages—so large that they can hardly carry them in their pockets, yet wages that will barely buy them the necessities of life. Then there are the middle classes, in their coffin-like homes, bare of furniture, fire, or any comfort. Theirs must be a curious experience—this waiting for an end, too weak even to complain or cast reproaches on their enemies. Typical of pre-war German docility is this patient expectation on the part of a class once so prominent and even wealthy —a class in which are contained all the journalists, writers, teachers, philosophers and brain-workers ; while in it are many authors of world-wide reputation now unable to eat meat more than once a month. But they realise what is in store for them. As one of the cartoonists wrote in *Simplicissmus*, "The German God is a merciful god, who will never forsake his people. He has, therefore, in his infinite mercy, allowed it to rain all this summer past, so that those who live on into the winter shall be accustomed to damp and cold." To them it is like living in a house which was formerly comfortable, but where one wall has completely disappeared and cannot be built up again. There is nothing to look at beyond it, nothing to hope for; only an infinite emptiness is there, out of which sometimes issues an icy wind, sweeping over the boundless flat plains of Asia, where the starving people die, and over the frozen steppes of the Russia that was called European. This wind lashes like a whip. Behind the other wall, to the south, is a race once the gayest, most charming of European peoples, but now suffering from something known as mass-hysteria—a nervous disease that arises from weakness, from eight or nine years of hunger, cold, and utter hopelessness — an epidemic never before known in the Modern World, a death-disease such as might afflict a beleaguered city after a long and terrible siege. This people, in spite of their intense suffering, are dying quietly—in the sense that they are too weak, too gentle, perhaps, to create any public disorder. But what will happen in Germany when starvation comes to the working man as well as to the middle classes? Mean-

A German Garden

while we read in the English papers such things as "A Fat Land—German Prosperity" or "Those Junkers Will Cheat You Yet." Yes, they probably will cheat us, and the whole country with them— cheat us as the middle classes have done already by starvation, by the endurance of every horror that can overwhelm an enlightened and once prosperous class, now left with nothing to clothe themselves in but the bitter wind from Russia— cheat us, too, by their ultimate disappearance. It is only in the country, in this peace and solidity of a traditional life, that any hope for the future seems to lie hidden. . . .

Meanwhile the rain having swept off to other conquests, we entered the garden that we had been waiting to see, astonished at its size and beauty. Meeting with but scanty mention of it in any guide-book, we had come expecting to find one which, though smaller, would resemble that other at Würzburg, three miles away. This latter was made for the same Prince-Bishop, a structure more than a garden, a vast ship of stone with trees growing on it, floating above the town, grandiose and beautiful, but in a cold, mechanical, too-logical way, that proclaimed it of French inspiration. But here was something rarer, possessing an imaginative quality not usually to be met with in these Northern climes, as Italian in character as the other is French.

In Germany, as in England, a style tends to

linger on after it has disappeared elsewhere. Thus mullioned windows are to be found in the Midlands built as lately as the first half of the eighteenth century, and in both countries the Gothic style died ever so slowly. In the same way we found before us an Italian formal garden, laid out after these havens of flowing water and blue shadow had ceased to be made in their own country, pointing, indeed, to what would have been the ultimate rococo development there, had not poverty and a change of taste cut short the great tradition. This garden at Voigtshochheim, created between the years 1755 and 1779, shows clearly its descent from such places as the Villa d'Este at Tivoli and the Villa Lante near Viterbo. But where in Italy would you find a garden of this kind built at so late a date? At Caserta, certainly, there is a formal lay-out, but it is one more influenced by the example of Versailles than by any of the Italian palaces. Then there is the Pisani garden at Stra; but that can hardly be called a formal one. For the rest, few gardens were made in Italy at this time; and those there are, were mostly made in the style so wickedly christened "*Giardino Inglese*," a conglomeration of plaster temples, weeping-willows, sham rocks, Greek bathing-pools, and groves of mangy tropical trees entirely unsuited to their environment, with an occasional bed of burnt-up but still triumphant red geraniums. Originally these places must have

A German Garden

been more hideous even than they are to-day when, if seen by the light of a sufficiently sentimental sunset, they disseminate a faint Chopinesque charm. This style of garden, still favoured by the Italians, culminates in various burial-grounds, so that, roughly, it can be said that after the year 1750 the Italian garden turned its back on the Villa D'Este and marched in the direction of the Cemetery at Genoa.

Voigtshochheim, therefore, is particularly interesting, in that it enables you to enter into a haunted land. It tells you what might have been, if various revolutions had not cut short the eighteenth century. It is like a photograph of a Napoleonic victory at Waterloo, and the story of its subsequent developments. As in many Italian examples, the house here is nothing, the garden everything. The greatest skill and ingenuity is shown in the planning; not an inch of ground is wasted: everything is part of an elaborate and—what is more important—of a beautiful scheme. Yet there is no effect of crowding, in spite of the numerous "stunts" imposed by German rococo taste : on the contrary there is shown a genuine sense of co-ordination and design. The natural features of the landscape can have offered little help to the garden-architect, for here are no steep slopes, ravines, hanging woods, or cascades.

Entering the garden down a long yew alley that cuts the space nearly in half, you are enticed

Discursions

toward the farther end by a charming statue in a high, green niche. But the hedge on your right opens out suddenly, revealing a large sheet of water. This oval lawn lies under the grey light like an old mirror, its rusty silver surface showing up where the floating masses of weeds touch the air, breaking the smoothness of the water. There are four slightly Chinese monsters rising out of this lake, guarding the middle of it, from which leaps up into the air, on four open arches through which the further water quivers, an immense tower of masonry. At each corner of this structure are stone shepherdesses, some playing mandolins with their stiff fingers, others gazing down into the depths; and high above them, from the top of the pedestal, rears a stone Pegasus, wings outstretched to fly. In the flat water beneath you can see him starting on his downward career of rushing wings, through long green alleys, their darkness only broken by the watery echo of a grey statue, down through the solemn wide paths, past the tall trees that reverse their circling green shadows.

Shallow flights of steps lead into this lake at regular intervals, and on each side of them are placed vases of stone fruit or flowers, or baskets in which lies a tortoise or a scaly fish. The whole sheet of water is enclosed by an old yew hedge, in which are sunk many statues, looking as if they had been drawn by one of the late Venetian artists

282

VOIGTSCHOCHHEIN : GARDEN FIGURE

A German Garden

—by Pittoni, Ricci, Piazzetta—and then transferred
into stone ; goddesses, in crumbling armour, under
helmets from which curl flowing plumes, sit quietly,
listening to the music of a Cupid, who, curled-up
at their feet, runs his fingers across a small
harp. Everywhere are statues, many more than
there are people in the village outside the gates,
enough to populate a town with dusky, moving
shadows ; on every hand are vistas of yew hedge,
leafy tunnel and silent fountain, for no water runs
in this deserted place. In the centre of the
garden rises a circle of vast plane-trees, whose
peeling bark gives a false sunshine even to the
dullest day. Motionless, beneath their low-sailing
branches, stands a sad group of gods and goddesses,
observing the growth of the great trees with a
never-changing look of disdain, for they remember
them when they were no higher than their own
pedestals. A different world it was then. But
now these green giants have outgrown them,
have, literally, put them in the shade, so that no
sunshine ever comes to thaw their old blood, to
warm their old limbs, nor any light save the false
tiger-like markings of the trees above, or cold
dripping circles like those at the bottom of a deep,
clear pool on a fine day.

There is a garden theatre too, and though the
statues have gone, though the theatre is empty
and desolate, a throbbing sound comes up from
the deep, green hollow laid for the orchestra, where

Discursions

the dusty bees can still warm themselves in a sheltered place. The high, domed shell-work grotto, two storeys in height, stands shuttered, so that one can only just peer, from a balcony above, into a darkness faintly skimmed by the fingers of the light, stealing in through green shutters.

Occasionally a window, cut in hedge or wall, reveals alley after alley, green depth after green depth; Chinese temples, looking like fungi, rise out of the ground, reminding one how late was this work, how nearly the last of formal gardens, how it verges, even, upon the Pagodenburg at Munich and the Pavilion at Brighton. But there is nothing eccentric about it. The whole effect is calm and restful. Yet when this garden was planned, the world was already shaping for itself a new era, an epoch in which Prince-Bishops are felt to be too ornamental and garden statues are made no more; an era, in fact, in which the only opportunity that comes to the sculptor is that of designing a memorial to commemorate his fallen brothers.

Wandering slowly through the green canals, we felt an atmosphere coming at us from the village. It was Saturday evening, and already that extraordinary feeling of Sunday was creeping over the world, ready for the next day—a feeling that stretches like a fog right over Northern Europe and, decidedly, touches other continents—America, Australia, and South Africa, probably penetrating

A German Garden

even into India. As we wandered through those
quiet alleys, toward the road, the guttural voices
of the passers-by burrowed through the thick
hedges, floating toward us. Separated still from
the world, it was possible to appreciate the characteristics of their speech. How inevitable it now
seemed that a people speaking thus should be
defeated by a race using such a language as the
French. How could this clumsy, strong, tactless,
rather kindly tongue ever dare to engage in
combat with the subtle, cold, neat, supple, well-
ordered one of the French people, who can express
every shade of feeling with the greatest precision,
and, at the same time, economy of words?
Consider even the construction of the German
sentence, the way in which the whole meaning is
propelled hopelessly to the end of it! Consider
their writing, as clumsy a form of lettering as
exists, and then compare it with French sentences,
French writing. But then how typical are all
languages. Spanish has the twang of the guitar
in it, the harsh taste of the wine of the country,
the acrid colouring of its landscape. The Italian
speech is flowery and full of sentiment, beautiful
in the same way as Tuscany or Umbria, yet
practical as its people. But above all others
does the English tongue express the national
temper and characteristics in its sound, its form,
its construction. We have more words for the
same thing than any other European language,

Discursions

in this being the exact reverse of the French. How often the same tendency expresses itself in the national life; when, for instance, we are at war with a nation, we find it necessary, perhaps from an innate kindliness, perhaps from other reasons, to invent a new name for our enemies. The French became "Froggies," the Germans "Huns." These nicknames enable us utterly to forget the virtues of our enemy, of which we were formerly cognisant, and thus render us more formidable as foes. At the same time the disguise is so complete that occasionally it defeats its own object. It is recorded that on the night of a severe air-raid in the late (Great) war an English cook remarked to her mistress during a session in the cellar: "It ain't the Germans, M'm, as I minds; it's them there 'Uns I can't abide!"

But directly the war is over these nicknames are forgotten, and with them disappears the hatred attached, not to a people, but to a name temporarily bestowed upon them. And it is in this same spirit that we deal with our old friends the sheep, the ox, and the pig. These dear, familiar figures of our rustic landscape become suddenly alien to us when engulfed by our human greed. That pet, very woolly sheep that so often makes its bow in those charming, simple country lyrics of Mr Y. ("I parleyed with a little lamb") becomes merely so much dead, very edible mutton. Those Highland cattle that Mr X. so often

A German Garden

rendered, wrapped round in a Scotch mist like a purple tulle scarf — that are still so eagerly sought by dentists and amateurs of mid-Victorian painting generally — are transformed, under the white muslin cover of the club sideboard, merely into so many portions of delicious cold beef. But then the whole English attitude toward animal-life is peculiar. It was in this country that the excellent work of the Society for the Prevention of Cruelty to Animals first originated. Yet, though the idea of this society was a noble one, though its work has been splendid, there is something a little illogical about it. We have yet to hear that the members of this association have given up a meat diet. What would our missionaries think if they heard that the cannibals and head-hunters of New Guinea had formed a society for the Prevention of Cruelty to Missionaries? They might even think it somewhat hypocritical. . . . We remember a cousin of ours who took a great pride in her garden, her orchard, her chickens. She fed the latter herself and was almost senti-mentally attached to them, bestowing upon them various pet-names, so that when she called one particular pullet it would run to her. Thus there was between them a real link of affection, and in her own mind she never associated these handsome birds with those pleasures of that table to which she was also attached. When the fatal day, the hour of execution, arrived, she would shed

Discursions

endless tears at the loss of her pet; yet never would the bird be reprieved, and directly the blow had fallen, her tears were dried. It simply became, then, a dead chicken like any other—and we should have excellent food for dinner the following night.

How, then, could a race accustomed to eat *Kalbsfleisch*, where we eat that abstract food from the gods called veal, to revel in such things as *Kalbskopf* and *Fünfminutenfleisch*, ever expect to defeat us by diplomatic or any other means? If defeat came our way, we should, as Napoleon said, simply not recognise it. We should call it by another name; for the mere fact that we have a familiar saying about "calling a spade a spade" goes to prove how often we call it something else.

iv

Sunday Afternoon

MUSING thus we drove back to Würzburg, paid our fare of five, six or seven thousand marks, and were deposited at the hotel. In front of this spreads an enormous paved square, flanked and faced by the Residenz, with its background of pheasant-coloured trees.

This huge stone palace, one of the biggest in Europe, is placed right in the middle of the town, the gardens and woods attached to it being bordered with miles of fine iron railing, occasionally broken by stone piers and superbly fantastic gates. Thus are obtained continual views, all through the town, of fountains, statues, green glades and tall trees. The whole town is dominated by the great structure of the Palace, built for two brothers, one succeeding the other in the capacity of Prince-Bishop, between the years 1720 and 1744. These brothers belonged to the family of the Counts Schönborn, and love of building must have been in their blood, for their family built, and still own, Pommersfelden, which has the reputation of being the most beautiful garden in Germany ; and themselves, besides creating the Residenz here, and numerous chapels

T   289

Discursions

and churches in the city, were responsible for the creation of that very interesting New Palace at Bamberg, and for the laying out of the garden at Voigtshochheim which we have just described. The plans for the Residenz were entrusted to J. B. Neumann, a native of the town and foremost German architect of his day. And most important of all, in the interior decoration the brothers employed the greatest Venetian artist then living; which tends to show that even if their building operations were inspired by an ostentatious love of display, the latter was at any rate informed by a real knowledge and appreciation of beauty.

To see paintings by a familiar and favourite artist in a place far from the usual field of his activities is one of the greatest pleasures of life. It gives you, immediately, a sense of comfort, prejudices you at once in favour of the house, the town even, that shelters them. It is as if you had met an old friend, whose presence redeems the place for you from any feeling of shyness or of being in a strange land. And if the artist stayed here, actually worked here, you know that the town is no barbarian place, but has felt the breath of the sacred fire.

That is the terrible thing about new countries! It does not matter, it is indeed an obvious advantage, to have no history—but how is it possible to admire these giant mountains, these colossal falls, the rugged beauty of a virgin land, when you know

Sunday Afternoon

quite well that no form of art has ever touched any spot in these vast tracts—and probably will not visit them very much for several centuries? But here in Würzburg you have (though a "Hunhater" wrote in a newspaper article the other day that the Residenz "displayed German Art at its fattest") the most important of all Tiepolo's frescoes, and immediately the town became—not a cold one of grey stone set in a hard northern light, but a pleasant annexe of Italy. The long arcades of the Piazza enfold you once more, and above you glint the velvet sky and keen eyes of the Venetian night. The Lion of St Mark, whose presence in any town on the mainland seems always to indicate that it is more charming, more comfortable and gayer than another town of its size lacking this emblem would be, extends here, too, his beneficent influence. You enter the vast world that Tiepolo has formulated, and immediately all the associations that his name evokes sound their varying music in your mind, join on to your new impressions. Verona, Venice, Milan, Udine, Madrid, all flash before you. Once again you float on those dusky, purple clouds of sunset, or on those fleecy, rosy ones that have so obviously evaporated from the snow-capped hills at the sun's first touch, over the head of the everyday world, in heroic company. Goddesses, of more than mortal beauty of flesh, ride with you on these journeys: white figures fan you with their cool wings, weed-crowned water-

Discursions

gods pour out their nectar from deep pitchers;
while a dwarf keeps watch on the globe below.
You will remember that palace in Milan, now a
dusty law court, where hidden away in a corner
is perhaps the most beautiful, as these at Würzburg are the most sumptuous, of Tiepolo's painted
rooms. The long, narrow, gilded saloon, with its
many windows on one side, and four great panels
of Flemish tapestry on the other, has over it a
coved ceiling on which is represented the Triumph
of the Sun. Apollo, in glory, is saluted by angels
whose wings are patterned like those of a butterfly, while elephants lift their trunks into the ceiling,
salaaming and trumpeting their admiration at him.

Then there is the Palazzo Labia. You will
recollect the turning off from the Grand Canal,
the Ghetto rising up on one side like so many
rocks pierced with caves, and on the other the
mouldering grey palace with its orange-tiled roof.
Through a high-pillared, desolate courtyard you
walk up a broad staircase. The key scratches for
a moment in its socket, and you enter the room.
Above your head musicians play on gourd-shaped
stringed instruments, or blow down long trumpets,
and you are again in that familiar atmosphere of
brocades, silk banners, feathers, gold and pearls,
of that luxuriant beauty which is so hard to
create. For just as the painter finds it most
difficult to make interesting, in terms of paint,
the study of a woman conventionally pretty, and

PRINCE-BISHOP'S PALACE, WÜRZBURG

Sunday Afternoon

indeed is apt to shirk the problem altogether (perhaps Renoir was the one artist of the last fifty years who was courageous enough to face and master this question), thus is it hardest, too, to make a work - of - art out of all these things so pretty, so rich in superficial loveliness. It is harder to combine them in a work-of-art, to get out of them a purely pictorial quality of beauty, than it is to make an interesting picture out of a basket of mixed vegetables or a Staffordshire china figure ; it is as difficult to distil out of them a purely æsthetic beauty as it is for a camel to go through the eye of a needle. And even if Tiepolo's art fell short of the greatest, in that it only sought to please—which must be the aim, after all, of any decorative painting—it must be remembered that it is probably easier to displease than to please, easier to be a good painter or a good decorator than to be both—and Tiepolo's work is the highest form of decorative painting. It is an art that could thrive only in a decadent - aristocratic age ; intended for the decoration of a palace as obviously as much modern art to be seen in schismatic exhibitions is intended for the beautifying of the interior of cottages in the garden-suburbs ; and is neither the better nor the worse for this. In addition, his work proves that he had two gifts which are usually understood to be dangerous ones, the greatest skill and a flowery imagination. As you look at this room you feel

Discursions

that the outward loveliness of life, the soft flowing of water, the sheen of mortal beauty, the rustling flash of silk brocades, the liquid movement of feathers and plumes, the crimson shadows cast by gold, the fleshly beauty of pearls, have never been realised and stated so completely before, not even by his great ancestor Veronese. Never before have these things kept their own beauty so well, and acquired a new, more permanent one. For there is something more here than the crystal husk of the fruit, or outward beauty reflected in a mirror. Again, as with the older masters, you are freed from this world, swept off to some fabulous land whose soft radiance, low-singing waves and murmur of stringed music, as of a serenade, shall haunt you for a lifetime. On the wall here, prodigal of her wealth, Cleopatra lets a pearl drop into a glass of wine, until its lustre dissolves into the amber glow, just as Tiepolo allows the brimming measure of his genius to flow even into things unworthy of it.

Then there is the Episcopal Palace at Udine, with its ceiling, and painted columns of twisted alabaster; the Villa Valmarano near Vicenza, with its suites of small painted rooms, where Harlequin and Punchinello peep out of their striped booths, where figures in cloaks and three-cornered hats watch the charlatans, masked like themselves, but with strange black beaks, strutting high up on their trestles. Looking up, they watch the movements

Sunday Afternoon

of these white-clad figures, which a modern poet has thus described:

" Two feathers in their hair
Comedians strut the sheer edge
Above the foaming crowd,
Loose sleeves and trousers flapping with the wind.
Through the crowd
The tremors of their movements run
Till the furthest feel,
Dashed in their faces
The fierce blossoms of each whistling parrot-cry."

In this same villa are the only *chinoiserie* paintings that Tiepolo ever carried out, showing an affinity to those Beauvais tapestries designed by Boucher.

Now the most extravagant monument of the Venetian eighteenth century spreads out before you as the Palazzo Pisani at Stra wakens in your memory — that vast building, echoed in only a slightly minor key at the other end of its formal canal. For the stables are nearly as monumental as the house itself. The gardens are full of tall trees, just breaking into leaf on this first fine day of the early spring, and the ground beneath is powdered with clusters of frail, hardly-open wild-flowers, white and blue: and among these, on little mounds splashed with wind-moving shadows, stone gods and goddesses play a Petit-Trianon-like game of shepherd and dairymaid. The ballroom which, after all the vicissitudes that the house has passed through, is now the only really interesting room in it, is a superb example of the art of this master. The walls are covered with painted architecture, designed, no doubt, not by the artist himself, but by an architectural painter whom he had trained and always employed. For as the patrician families in Venice had invariably ruined themselves over the building of their palaces before they had even considered the interior decoration, this magician could give Tiepolo his necessarily splendid background of arches, pillars of alabaster or marble, and overhanging galleries from which imagined music would pour down, in a manner that was much more real than the actual things, and infinitely cheaper. Tiepolo was, then, always accompanied by this anonymous artist, and usually by his son, Domenico, who inherited a part of his father's genius. By the younger one are those panels and that ceiling, formerly the decoration of a casino on the mainland, now in the possession of the Museo Correr at Venice. Many Punchinellos, clothed in their loose white garb, with black masks, beaked like birds of prey, walk on tight-ropes over your head or at your side. They walk, balance, revolve on these taut strings, fall through the sparkling blue air like so many birds, uttering shrill cries that flash down at you, brilliant as their own white garments. Occasionally the dark green branch of one of those fir-trees, that are so plentiful in the neighbourhood of the Brenta,

Sunday Afternoon

obtrudes itself into the picture, otherwise there is
nothing to interfere with the hard blue vacancy
of the sky and the line of those balancing, snowy
figures. Out of these the artist contrives to get
an almost abstract quality.

By Domenico, too, is that series of more than
a hundred drawings, illustrating the life of Punchinello, perhaps the most typical work of this period,
which was sold at Sotheby's two or three years
ago, and is now to be seen in the Musée des Arts
Décoratifs at the Louvre. Probably he helped his
father decorate the ballroom of this palace at Stra ;
on the ceiling of the room, with its radiant golden
colouring and hanging chandeliers of gilded wood,
is shown the Apotheosis of the Pisani family. The
Procurator, who was really rather a disreputable
old man, is being received by his numerous virtues
in a heathen heaven, while, under the lunettes,
satyrs, painted in gold and grisaille, watch his
pompous arrival in this unexpected place with a
sly leer of surprise.

This palace has other curious links with the
history of painting, for it was here that the old
King and Queen of Spain, so often both the
patrons and victims of Goya's marvellous art, spent
a part of their lives in semi-captivity, hither trans-
ported, like innocent babes, by the Napoleonic
eagles. Here poor simple old Charles IV., whom
Goya always presents to us as on his way to hunt
or to shoot, pined in a sham liberty. Of a very

Discursions

affectionate disposition, he adored all his family, and constantly sent imploring messages to his odious brother, Ferdinand of Naples, asking him to come over to Stra. But Ferdinand was too busily employed in making advances to the Duchess de la Floridia even to give a thought to his Royal brother in exile. The latter at last preferred to seek the actual and open want of personal liberty imposed by monastic rules; and ended his life in a convent near Rome. The old Queen, with her deep-set eyes, flowing black mantilla, and that peculiarly horrible look of aged coquetry which Goya always takes particular care to accentuate, and which gave her the dreadful air of a dancing skeleton dressed in the liveliest fashion, must have found her life all the harder because of a disposition more active than that of her husband. It would, incidentally, be interesting to know what Maria Luisa thought of all these portraits of herself by Goya. What did they convey to her? One can understand her employing the artist once — by mistake—but that she should have allowed this cruel realist to become practically the Court painter is inexplicable. Either she must have possessed a love of art that surmounted all obstacles, blinding her even to the ridicule thrown upon herself, or Goya's personal charm must have been so great as to hypnotise her. No Royal Personage, no President, would allow "such a thing" to be painted nowadays. At any rate, the Queen must

Sunday Afternoon

be forgiven much for the sake of her many portraits, and it is sad to think of her in this ballroom, mocked by a ceiling which must have recalled to her the palace in Madrid, with its even more magnificent frescoes by Tiepolo. As she gazed at this triumph, these flying figures, satyrs, and roseate clouds, there must have come back to her in detail all the splendour of her dead life, the pomp and etiquette attached to the persons of the reigning monarchs in Spain; and the Pisani palace itself must have seemed a simple, unluxurious home.

Then, as the memory of Stra grows dim, many of Tiepolo's smaller pictures come back to you. There are those two paintings of Rinaldo and Armida at Munich; there is that Venus at Trieste, most beautiful of all his smaller works, swaying gently in her amber conch, inborne by racing green tides. All these, like Cleopatra's pearl, dissolve into the general golden glow induced in your mind, as you look up here in the Residenz at the whole world created and evoked by this great master. The stone double-staircase, enormous in itself, balustraded and set with statues, glides up into the air almost imperceptibly, till you find yourself standing on the wide landing, or walking round the gallery that encircles it. But all these vast spaces are dwarfed by the expanse of ceiling above. It is incredible that this whole world of light and shadow, of the silken flash of flowing water, of brocades, bellied

Discursions

out like sails, of these palm-trees, their leaves up-lifted, swirling like plumes, by an invisible southern breeze, can be the work of one man! Some giant, some demigod must have breathed life into this new creation of mortals and immortals. The medal-like effigy of the Prince-Bishop, in his long curling periwig, is wafted up into the dome of dawnlit air by a flying cloud of nymphs, angels, and cherubs, who, trumpet to mouth, blow their golden fanfares straight down upon you. The dawn is just beginning; its chariot and four white horses thunder like waves over you, till the whole earth is alight, though a rainbow attempts to circum-scribe its glory. From above the four vast walls of this building, the four quarters of the globe rise to meet the first glow of morning. Asia, with her love of splendour, displays her silks, pearls, jewels, state-umbrellas and all those other objects in which the Venetian artists, too, most Oriental of all Europeans, could revel. Here are dusky Indians, tall Turks with scimitars and turbans, Chinamen yellow and cruel as gold, elephants in Durbar-dress, their trunks lifted up in salaam, while monkeys peer out from the jungle background. Africa, opposite, is an ancient world re-born, a world free of the white man, the Africa of Egypt and Carthage, of a wealth and learning that are legendary; tall negresses, crowned with ostrich feathers, stand up proudly among tropical flowers; near by them a tall

Sunday Afternoon

ostrich raises his silly head into the air, and many rainbow-coloured birds have left the forest to watch this artist at his work. Palm-trees let their broad leaves sail calmly on the warm air, and an enormous crocodile, with scaly skin, an armour like that of some prehistoric monster, is coming up out of the river bed, restrained by its master, the River-God of the Nile, old and white as Time himself, and crowned with damply-glistening green weeds. Europe, the Christian continent, rises up with the Cross and the Triple Tiara, while a figure, probably the Holy Roman Emperor, receives tribute from the kneeling figures of Commerce, Justice, Learning, the Arts, and all those symbolic figures, refugees now in other continents. Then America is shown, a world as it would have been without the civilising influence of the Inquisition in the South and of the Non-conformist Conscience in the North, a civilisation akin to Venice and the East, a land of dusky figures crowned with high plumes, looking unafraid into the golden mirror of the future, against its ancient, unruined background of obelisks, pyramids, and cyclopean buildings—an America that has progressed on its own traditional lines, or recovered its individuality again,

" Till the freed Indians in their native groves
Reap their own fruits, and woo their sable loves ;
Peru once more a race of kings behold
And other Mexicos be roofed with gold."

Discursions

As we walked away, we looked up to see a dwarf edging away, down out of the ceiling, obviously on the point of leaving his world of frozen action and coming to join us in our journey through the endless suites of the palace. Most of these rooms were redecorated between 1800 and 1820 and are very fine examples of that period. There are still, however, a few untouched rooms of the original epoch, notably a room, the ceiling and walls of which are encrusted with mirror set in irregular pieces of gilding, and painted with little designs of fruit and flowers; a most fantastic apartment, which even in the half-light of closed shutters and draped curtains had a golden sheen like that which shows inside a gold bowl. It was, however, difficult to see the rooms, for the old spirit of the German army still survives—only survives—unbroken by any misfortune or national calamity — in the guardians of this palace, square-headed, wearing round caps like those of Burke and Hare, and other early nineteenth - century murderers to be seen at Madame Tussaud's, moustached like Hindenburg, while in their boots is the whole heaviness of a large nation. These gentlemen regard it as their only duty to insist that the windows are muffled up, that no light shall penetrate into the regions where they reign, and, generally, to prevent the visitor from getting near enough to any object to see it properly. Adamant are they, strong and energetic in the performance of these

Sunday Afternoon

welcome duties. There is a magnificent ballroom-
like marble chapel, with two or three rather uninteresting sacred pictures by Tiepolo; and there
is a room, well guarded by a Cerberus more than
usually Tirpitz-like in appearance, with three large
and very beautiful panels of tapestry, designed by
a Frenchman named Perrot, and representing
Carnival scenes at Venice; the only tapestries of
their kind we have ever seen. Under arcades,
covered with those large leaves and flowers which
only grow in woven gardens, with a background of
canals, towers, and domes, all these fantastic people
feast among huge vases of sunflowers and roses,
gigantic baskets of ripe melons, peaches, and grapes.
There is another scene laid in the Piazzo San
Marco. But all these three panels have that
dream-like quality peculiar to tapestry: a dim
green or blue light pervades them, as if we walked
in some submarine city; the trees, flowers—all the
foliage—are anemones or trailing weeds; the bowls
of fruit are turned to coral and sea-shells; the
Venetian palaces, already belonging to the ocean,
become mansions of mother-of-pearl or gigantic
shapes of the sea seen dimly through the water
that lies between them and the onlooker. The
people who flaunt along these cool corridors are
more nearly related to mermen than to human
beings; the masked comedian who blows down a
trumpet is transformed into a triton, and light like
salt-foam falls over him, and over all the scene,

303

Discursions

while the music that sounds is that of the small waves heard in the hollow of a shell.

Leaving this tapestry, we pass again into the hard realism of the First Empire. Then, in the middle of this vast palace, overlooking the central point of its garden, we enter the Kaisersaal. This high, two-storeyed room was intended by the Prince-Bishops for the reception of the Holy Roman Emperor when he visited them on his way to and from Vienna. And here, at last, the wealth of the Church gave Tiepolo the background that had, usually, to be made for him in counterfeit. The customary arches, marble pillars and doorways are this time not the magic practised by a very clever architectural painter, but as solid and substantial as they seem. The room is octagonal, oval in shape, with a high, coved ceiling broken by four lunettes. The sides of it are set with marble pillars, bearing gilded capitals of a rococo design. Between these pillars are the niches of marble gods and goddesses, while crystal chandeliers sail low down into the air. The general effect is a radiant one of light colour, as if we found ourselves inside an immense casket of pearl. Above these two sets of marble pillars, beneath the gilded, sculptured folds of two very theatrical stucco - curtains, are two scenes representing the marriage of Frederick Barbarossa to Beatrix of Burgundy— which took place at Würzburg in 1156. One

KAISER'S HALL, WÜRZBURG. (FRESCOES BY TIEPOLO)

Sunday Afternoon

panel shows the Prince - Bishop blessing the wedded couple, who kneel to him, while the other depicts the prelate kneeling to his Emperor beneath a canopy held up by two huge green statues, like the haunting arc in *Don Giovanni*, or those in the last picture of Titian, at the Accademia in Venice. The page, holding the bishop's robe, is looking down into the room, and we can almost hear the whispering of a group of men in the corner. In the first panel there is a background of painted arches, through which we can distinguish a gallery full of people, eagerly watching the ceremony. Behind the kneeling couple, attendants carry banners bearing their coats-of-arms. Both of these panels, indeed the whole of the painting in this throne-room, show Tiepolo in his most masterly mood. Above, on the ceiling, is a triumphant riot of chariots, white horses, and flying figures, while under one of the lunettes a drummer beats on his kettle-drum. This sound, associated with processions and the pomp of life, throbs through the room, through the pearl-like air, seeming to galvanise the figures into action; it echoes out into the gardens, seen through the long windows—gardens which, with their spreading flights of stone steps, fountains, and balustraded terraces, rising like the decks of a ship one above the other, crowned with green tunnels and the regular shapes of yew and pleached alley, seemed to take on the legendary atmosphere of the room, to be part of the

Discursions

background of this Barbarossa, transformed here from a warrior into the hero of a fairy story, and of his flying company of immortals. Even the gods and goddesses have stepped out of the ceiling to rest in the cool shade of a green niche, and have there been struck into grey stone. Leaving the palace, we walked down into the enticing perspective of the garden. But directly we entered it, we noticed some subtle change. Was it merely that the magic of the room, when we had stood in it, had given the garden some quality it did not possess, or did something now intervene between us and the prospect, something grey and intangible? The day seemed still bright with a pebble-like hardness and roundness; the statues, the terraces, were still there, yet the air seemed, in an indefinable way, to be woolly, though the sky was blue, the water clear. . . . What was it, this thing? We had been bewitched by the Venetian, and had forgotten. . . . It was Sunday Afternoon!

Even in Germany, where the whole country rocks from day to day, where nothing is certain, nothing secure, this shadow manifests itself. It stretches a gaunt arm right over Northern Europe, it clutches the Atlantic. From Canada it passes through the United States, across the Pacific, to Australia and New Zealand, through the Dutch Islands and the Archipelago up to India, Aden, and Egypt. It has entrenched itself in Malta,

Sunday Afternoon

and appears like a wraith at the very gates of the Mediterranean.

In Germany, perhaps, it gives a little comfort, making us feel that there is a foundation of custom that cannot be broken. It takes away the beauty of life, but makes the earth solid, the air almost visible. Anywhere, waking out of sleep, coming, even, out of a long period of unconsciousness, we should have known instinctively that this was the first day of the week. Nor does it seem merely to be a mental quality of our own with which we have endowed inanimate things. It appears to have a very real objective existence. Each house, each street, the very landscape, wears its Sunday look. Who can solve this mystery? We look to Professor Einstein who has already solved problems as difficult. Meanwhile Tiepolo had disposed of it with the flame of his genius, and perhaps of all painters he is the best with whom to pass a Sunday Afternoon.

Appendix

Music

From " The Constitution of Fiume "

" Clause LXIV.

In the Italian Regency of the Carnaro, music is a religious and social institution.

Every one thousand years, every two thousand years there is born of the depths of the soul of the people a hymn, which is perpetuated.

A great people is not only a people that creates its God after its own image, but one which also creates its hymn for its God.

If every new-birth of a noble race is a lyrical effort, if every unanimous and creative sentiment is a lyrical power, if every new order is a lyrical order in the fullest acceptation of the word, then music considered as a ritual language is the exalter of the act of life and of the work of life.

Does it not seem that great music announces each time to the attentive and anxious multitude the kingdom of the spirit?

The kingdom of the human spirit has not yet commenced.

' When matter operating on matter can take the place of men's hands, then will the spirit commence to perceive the dawn of its liberty,' said a native

309

Appendix

of the Adriatic, a Dalmatian : the blind prophet of Sebenico.

Just as the cock's crowing hastens the dawn, so music hastens the aurora, that aurora : *Excitat auroram.*

In the meantime, in the instruments of labour and gain and of play, in the noisy machinery, for this likewise follows the precise rhythm like poetry, music finds its movements and its abundance.

Of its pauses is formed the silence of the tenth Corporation.

Clause LXV.

In all the Communes of the Regency there are choral and orchestral societies formed, which are subsidised by the State.

At the Edile College in the City of Fiume, orders have been given for the erection of a Rotunda capable of accommodating at least an audience of ten thousand people, which Rotunda is provided with convenient tiers for the listeners and an extensive well for the orchestra and the chorus.

The great choral and orchestral festivals are 'quite free,' as has been said by the fathers of the Church of the grace of God.

STATUTUM ET ORDINATUM EST (Thus established and ordained).

IURO EGO (I swear).

GABRIELE D'ANNUNZIO."